4.75

FUNCTIONING IN BUSINESS

P. Lance Knowles and Francis Bailey

Longman
London and New York

Longman Group UK Ltd.
Longman House, Burnt Mill, Harlow
Essex CM20 2JE, England
and Associated Companies throughout the world

Published in the United States of America by Longman Inc., New York

First published 1987
Third impression 1988

British Library Cataloguing in Publication Data
Knowles, P. Lance
Functioning in business.
1. English language—Text-books for
foreign speakers   2. English language—
Business English
I. Title   II. Bailey, Francis
428.2′4′02465   PE1128
ISBN 0-582-85267-6

Library of Congress Cataloging in Publication Data
Knowles, P. Lance.
Functioning in business.
1. English language—Business English.   2. English
language—Text-books for foreign speakers.   I. Bailey,
Francis.   II. Title.
PE1115.K67 1987   428.2′4′02465   86-15266
ISBN 0-582-85267-6

Set in Monophoto Photina 747, 11/13pt
Produced by Longman Group (FE) Ltd
Printed in Hong Kong

ISBN 0-582-85267-6

CONTENTS

The **Answer Key** is a separate supplement in the back of the book.

Preface

This text was developed over three years working with students in the intensive English program at the Language Institute of Japan. Our need was to improve our program in two areas: language functions useful for managing simple conversations in business, and listening comprehension. Though there were ample materials available for intermediate and advanced learners, we were not satisfied with existing materials designed for upper basic and pre-intermediate learners.

Our working assumptions were as follows:

1. language should be in context, preferably in a developing story of interest to adult learners, especially those involved in business;
2. at pre-intermediate levels, listening activities should play an especially important role in promoting language acquisition;
3. students should move from recognition and comprehension to *eventual* production and acquisition;
4. language functions and simple routines should be systematically recycled throughout the materials;
5. written follow-up exercises should help students recognize key phrases and should require listening for comprehension, first for gist and then for details.

With these assumptions as our guide, we identified what we felt to be the key language functions appropriate for pre-intermediate learners. We then developed a story within which these functions would naturally occur. Once the story took shape, we asked members of our staff to role-play and tape the situations (with no script). The results had an authentic quality that found positive acceptance by our students, so we were on our way.

Though the language level of the material seemed high at first, we isolated the points in each unit which caused difficulty and designed pre-listening and other exercises to guide students through the rough spots. We also added the introductory unit as a means to reduce the learning load. During the role plays it became clear which functions the students needed work on, and gradually, as students progressed through the text, our target phrases came to be incorporated into student speech. At the same time, much of the vocabulary which had seemed difficult for the students in the first episodes was steadily acquired, so that the text became easier (requiring less class time) as the term progressed. This allowed us to increase the difficulty of the variations. Used in this way, student progress was clear to both students and teachers, and the materials evolved into an integrated course, not just a series of unrelated lessons.

Acknowledgement

We would like to thank the following people for their participation in the making of the tapes: Brian Tobin, Laura Mayer, Michael Curtin, Dave Pickles, Chris Dickinson, and Naoko Seto.

We would like to thank the entire staff of the Language Institute of Japan for their support and encouragement throughout this project. In particular, we would like to thank Meg Grace, Paul Lehnert, Ellen Dussourd, Andy Gates, Duncan Macintyre, Kathy Maston, and Larry Riesberg.

Finally, we would like to thank Robert O'Neill and Steven Krashen, whose somewhat differing views influenced us in the preparation of these materials.

Lance Knowles (Consulting Director, Language Institute of Japan)
Francis Bailey (Academic Supervisor, Language Institute of Japan)

USING THE COURSE

Rationale

This short text is for upper basic/pre-intermediate students preparing to use English in a business context. In addition to basic vocabulary and concepts, it is important at this stage to develop a working knowledge of essential language functions (e.g. requesting, suggesting, refusing, etc.), without which it is almost impossible to manage even a simple conversation. The approach taken here is to develop students in two areas; recognition of key functional phrases, and production of key functional phrases. By 'recognition' we mean that students comprehend the message or intent of a phrase but may not be able to generate that phrase for spoken production. We use 'production' to mean that students can do both. In order to develop proficiency in both areas, key phrases are recycled from unit to unit and in a variety of situations.

The second major area of focus is on listening, both for general meaning and for specific items of information. Units are organized into pre-listening, general listening, and detailed listening sections, all based on unscripted tape material. Once these sections have been completed, students will have an understanding of the contextualized content of the conversations. With this as a base, a role play shifts the focus of the unit from information and content to how the conversation itself is actually managed, and to the key functional phrases.

The third aim of this text is to build a basic business vocabulary. Terminology specific to particular technical fields is avoided as much as possible, our aim being to concentrate on recycling high-frequency items that are essential in general business conversations. The core vocabulary of the book is introduced in the introductory unit, and is then recycled so that the book becomes increasingly easy as students progress.

The Materials

Each unit consists of a series of exercises (accompanied by a taped episode) that proceeds from Story Update and Pre-listening (Section A) to General Comprehension and Detailed Listening (Sections B and C). These sections establish the basic information and context of each Episode and are preparatory for a reconstruction Role Play (Section D). In the role play, students demonstrate both their comprehension of the total situation and their ability to use appropriate functional phrases from previously acquired language. This is followed up by a Functional Phrases cloze (Section E) which focuses on a mixture of familiar and new phrases that students are asked to recognize and fill in. The Supplementary Exercises (Section F) include the same or similar phrases in a scripted tape accompanied by a variety of listening and speaking exercises.

Once the teacher and students are used to the format, an entire unit can be completed in about an hour, either in two shorter lessons or in one long lesson. For very basic classes, more time can be spent on each section, in which case two 40-minute lessons are sufficient for each unit.

This material can also be used for self-study or in the language laboratory. Use of the material in this way develops listening comprehension and an ability to recognize various functional phrases. However, student involvement in the material may be less for lack of an opportunity to do the role plays.

The Answer Key in the back of the book includes answers to the General Comprehension and Detailed Listening Sections, the transcripts of the Episode dialogs and of the variations. The functional phrases used in the dialogs and the answers to Sections B and C are printed in bold type.

The Cassette Tape

The recordings of the Episode dialogs include the hesitations and interjections of ordinary, informal speech (these hesitations are included in the transcripts in the Answer Key). The speech is 'authentic' and delivered at normal speed. In the variation dialogs the aim has been to achieve clarity rather than authenticity. For listening practice, as wide a variety of voices as possible has been used throughout the tape.

Step-by-Step Instructions

1. Begin with the introductory unit. This introduces much of the vocabulary and story background necessary for subsequent units. The tape transcript for each section and answers for the comprehension questions are included within the Answer Key.

2. Story Update
    This can be read aloud by the teacher or played on the tape. The discussion questions help students focus on important points in the overall story (5–10 minutes).

3. Section A
    These questions should be answered *before* listening to the Episode on the tape. The main purpose is to introduce important vocabulary and familiarize students with the situation (5 minutes).

4. Section B
    Play the tape of the Episode and then ask students to do the True/False exercise (2–3 minutes). It is advisable not to check the answers until after the next section is completed.

5. Section C
    Play the tape of the Episode section by section, and more than once when necessary, so that the detailed questions can be answered or filled-in. After this is completed, both general comprehension and detailed listening questions can be corrected (see Answer Key) and discussed if necessary (8–12 minutes).

Because the emphasis of this text is on functions, the preparatory portions of each unit are intended to be gone through quickly. Story Update and Pre-listening should take no more than 10–15 minutes (once the class is familiar with the format). The

General Comprehension and Detailed Listening sections are preparatory for the Role Play.

6.   Role Play
     (1) Have students work in pairs or small groups. They should reconstruct the situation in a problem-solving fashion while the teacher monitors and supplies necessary assistance (5–10 minutes).
     (2) Choose students who did well in the small group practice to role-play the situation before the entire class (5 minutes). It is also possible to select one or two students from different groups to role-play the situation with the teacher. This kind of variation insures that participants in the role plays move away from rote-memorization towards listening and trying to respond appropriately.

7.   Section E
     Have students listen again to the tape of the Episode, line by line, to fill in the appropriate phrases. (In the first six Episodes the functional phrases are listed in boxes at the end of each section.) This can be done in class, in the language lab, or as homework (see Answer Key; 5–10 minutes).

8.   Section F
     The instructions for each unit vary and are indicated in the text and on the tape (10 minutes).

9.   Section G
     The follow-up role plays can be done in the same way as indicated above (10–15 minutes).

Introduction

This is the story of an important business trip. It begins with two companies. They are Yamashita Limited and Advanced Technologies. Here is information about these two companies. Listen to the tape and look at the pictures below. Mark the sentences below each picture true (T) or false (F).

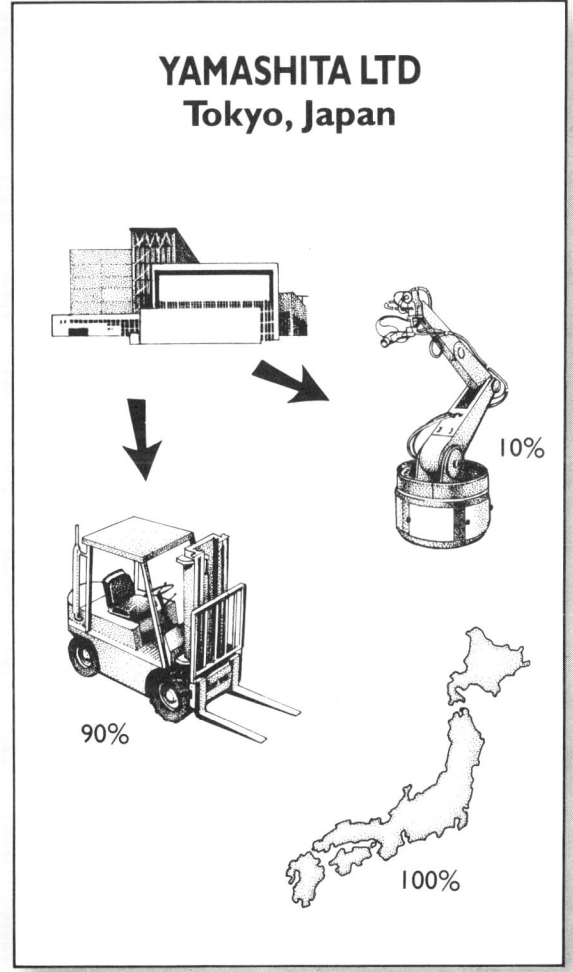

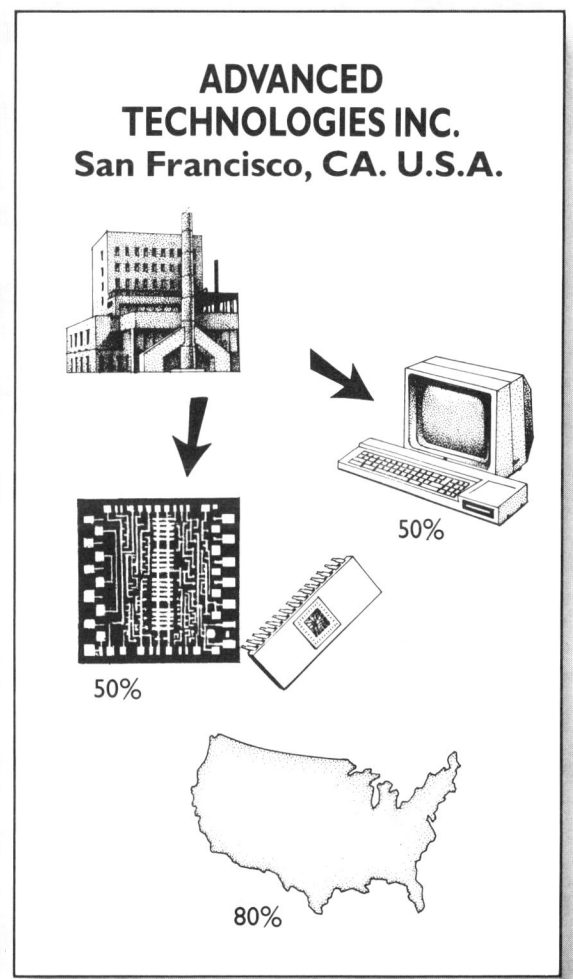

Comprehension

1. Yamashita manufactures automobiles.
2. Yamashita exports many industrial robots.

1. Advanced Technologies manufactures electronic components.
2. All of its products are sold in the U.S.

11

PART 2

The main characters in this story are Charles Blake and Mike Epstein. Here is information about them. Look at the pictures, and listen to the tape. Mark the sentences below each picture true (T) or false (F).

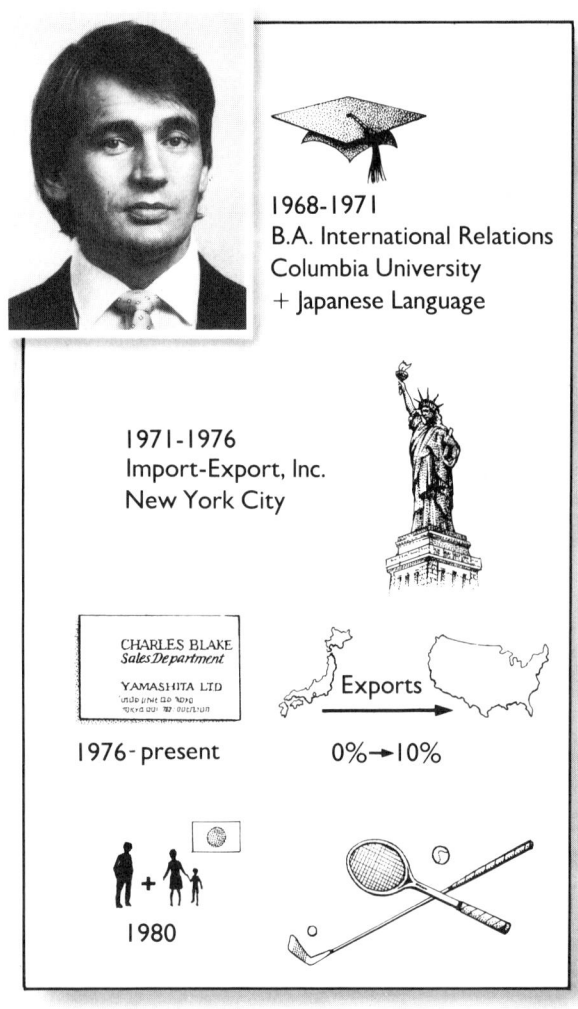

Comprehension

1. Mr. Blake is an engineer.
2. Mr. Blake works in New York.
3. Mr. Blake is married.
4. Mr. Blake works for a Japanese company

1. Mr. Epstein is an engineer.
2. Mr. Epstein works in San Francisco.
3. Mr. Epstein is married.
4. Mr. Epstein works for a Japanese company.

PART 3

The story began two months ago, in April. Here is more information about the story. Listen to the tape and look at the picture below. Mark the sentences below each picture true (T) or false (F).

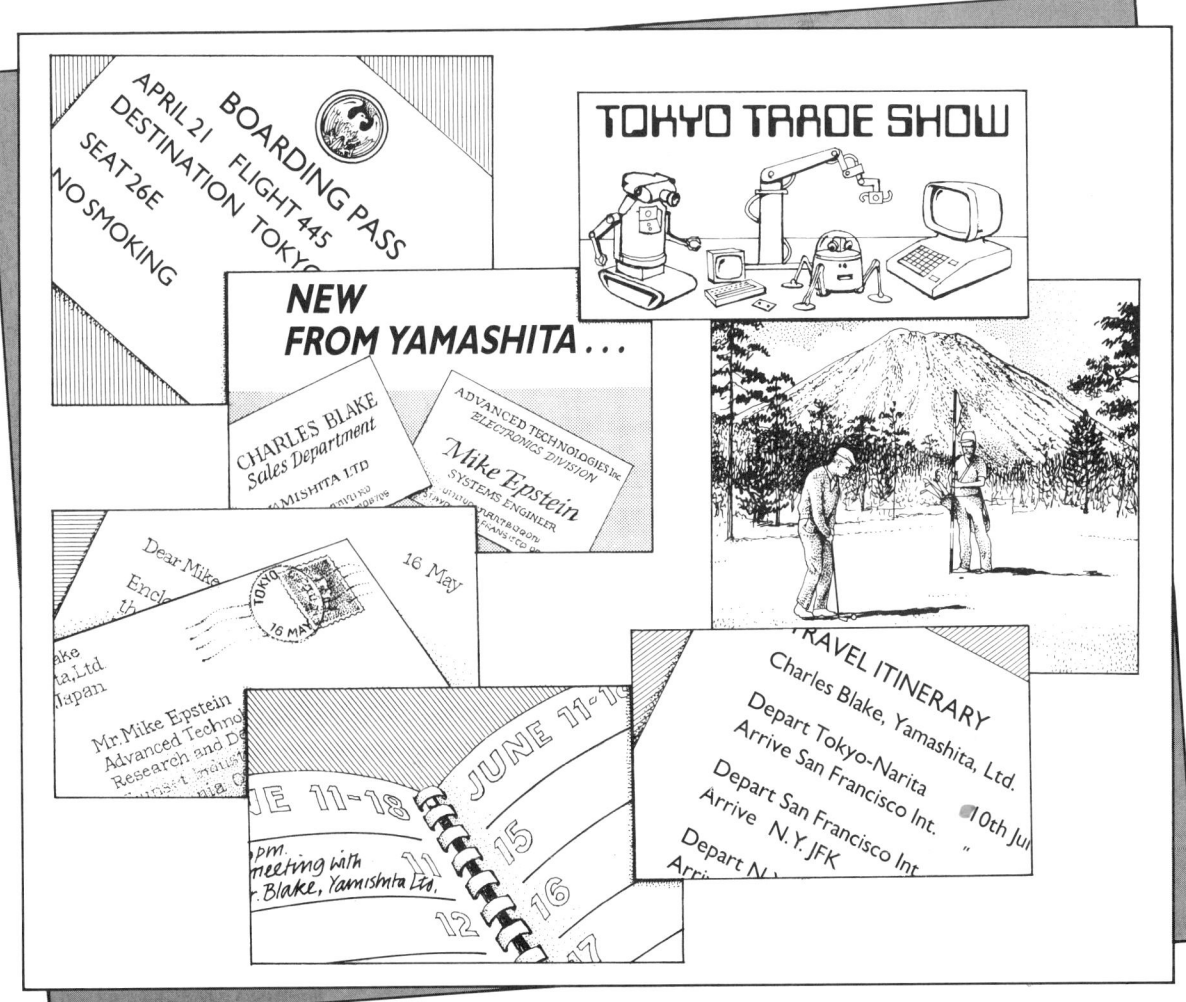

Comprehension

1. Mr. Epstein went to Japan on vacation.
2. Mr. Blake is going to come to San Francisco.
3. Mr. Epstein and Mr. Blake are going to meet in San Francisco.

Review the vocabulary in this unit. Then go on to Episode 1.

EPISODE 1

Checking In

STORY UPDATE

It is Monday, June 10th. Mr. Blake, from Yamashita Ltd., is in San Francisco. He wants to meet with Mr. Epstein of Advanced Technologies. Mr. Blake arrived in San Francisco this afternoon on a flight from Tokyo, Japan. He is now checking in to the San Francisco Hilton Hotel. It is 4:15 in the afternoon.

Discussion Questions

1. What company does Mr. Blake work for?
2. Why is Mr. Blake in San Francisco?

Scene Description   Charles Blake is at the Hilton Hotel in San Francisco. He is going to check in to the hotel.

A. Pre-listening

You are traveling alone on a business trip to the United States. You want to check in to a hotel. Indicate how you usually solve each of the following problems. (Rank the choices from 1–4 to indicate the order of your preferences.)

1.   You book your hotel room

    a.   with a confirmed reservation by a travel agency.
    b.   by personal letter.
    c.   by calling from the airport.
    d.   when you arrive at the hotel.

2.   The kind of room you usually stay in is a

    a.   single.
    b.   twin.
    c.   double.
    d.   suite.

3.   When you check in, the first thing you want to confirm is

    a.   the check-out time.
    b.   the room rates.
    c.   how you will pay.
    d.   if you have any messages.

4.   You usually pay by

    a.   cash.
    b.   personal check.
    c.   traveler's check.
    d.   major credit card.

5.   The most popular international credit cards in your country are

    a.   Visa.
    b.   American Express.
    c.   Master Card.
    d.   another kind of credit card.

Now listen to the tape.

B. General Comprehension

Mark the sentences true (T) or false (F).

1. Charles Blake has a reservation for the hotel.   T/F
2. The hotel clerk could not find Mr. Blake's reservation.   T/F
3. The reservation is for one night only.   T/F
4. Mr. Blake would like to pay with cash.   T/F
5. Mr. Blake wants to leave a day early.   T/F

C. Detailed Listening

Listen to the tape again. Fill in the answers below.

1. Charles Blake's confirmed reservation number is _____

2. He plans to stay at the hotel from Monday, June _____ through _____ June _____

3. The room costs _____ a night.

4. Charles Blake plans to pay by _____

5. Charles Blake might want to stay _____ night at the hotel but

   unfortunately the hotel is _____ for that night.

D. Role Play

Work in pairs. Take turns role-playing parts A and B below. The situation is the same as above. Then listen to the tape again and go on to the next exercise.

Part A
The time and place are the same as above. Your reservation number is 14689, and you want to stay an extra night. You want to stay until Saturday, June 15th. Please check in.

Part B
You are the receptionist at the San Francisco Hilton Hotel. Please help A, who has reserved a room through Thursday night. The hotel is fully booked on Friday.

E. Functional Phrases

Listen to the tape, line by line. Write the correct phrase from the list at the end of the section.

1. Offering, Agreeing, and Confirming

   Clerk: Good evening sir. Welcome to the San Francisco Hilton.

   _____

Blake: Yeah, my name is Blake, Charles Blake. I have a confirmed reservation.

....

Clerk: . . . That's for June 10th through the 13th, Monday through Thursday night.
          _____, sir?

Blake: _____

| Yes, that's fine. | Is that correct . . . | Can I help you? |

---

2.   Requesting, Agreeing, Refusing, Promising

Clerk: That room is $95 a night, sir.

Blake: Okay, fine. _____ use my American Express card for that?

Clerk: _____ sir. Uh, _____ do a
          print of your card before we check you in here?

....

Blake: Oh, by the way, there's a chance that I will be staying one more day, uh, so I
          might be leaving on Saturday. _____

Clerk: Uh, let me check. Well sir, _____ we're all booked up for
          Friday night, but something may open up. I can let you know.

Blake: Okay, _____ let me know as soon as possible,
          _____

Clerk: Yes, sir, _____ do that for you. Here's your key, sir. Bellman, front!

| Can I . . . | we'll . . . | if you could _____ I would appreciate it.* |
| can I . . . | Is that okay? | I'm afraid . . .   Yes, certainly . . . |

---

*Note: 'Could you . . .' can be used in place of 'If you could _____ I would appreciate it.'
However, the second phrase is less direct and more polite than the first phrase.*

F. Supplementary Exercises

VARIATION: Cashing a check

General Comprehension Questions

Listen to the tape and answer the questions below.

1. Can the customer change British pounds for American dollars?   Yes/No
2. Can the customer cash a personal check?   Yes/No
3. Can the customer see the manager?   Yes/No
4. Does the customer agree to see the Assistant Manager, Ms. Grace?   Yes/No

Functional Phrases

Listen to the tape again and fill in the exact words.

Bank Teller: _____

Customer: Yes. _____ change British pounds for American dollars here?

Bank Teller: Yes, certainly sir. How much would you like to change?

Customer: One hundred pounds please. Also, _____ cash a personal check from my London Bank?

Bank Teller: _____ that isn't possible. Our policy is that we do not cash out of town checks.

Customer: It's very important that I cash this check . . .

Bank Teller: Yes, I understand, but the bank policy . . .

Customer: _____ see the manager please?

Bank Teller: _____ the manager, Mr. Grover, is out right now. The Assistant Manager, Ms. Grace is in. Would that be all right?

Customer: _____ Thank you.

Bank Teller: Certainly. One moment please.

Could I . . .	I'm afraid . . .	May I help you?
could I . . .	I'm sorry but . . .	Yes. That's fine.
Can I . . .		

EPISODE 2

Making an Appointment

STORY UPDATE

Mr. Blake is now at the Hilton Hotel in San Francisco. He checked in to the hotel a few minutes ago. Now he wants to make an appointment with Mr. Mike Epstein, of Advanced Technologies. He wants to make the appointment for tomorrow, Tuesday, June 11th. Mr. Epstein knows Blake's schedule and is expecting his call.

Discussion Questions

1. Who does Mr. Blake want to see?

2. When does Mr. Blake hope to see Mr. Epstein?

3. Why does Mr. Epstein want to see Mr. Blake?

Scene Description   It is now the afternoon of June 10th. Mr. Blake is in his hotel room. He is going to call Mr. Epstein at Advanced Technologies to arrange an appointment for tomorrow morning.

A. Pre-listening

Rank the choices from 1–3.

1. Mr. Blake is going to telephone Mr. Epstein. What do you think they will discuss?

    a.   purpose of the meeting
    b.   time and place of the meeting
    c.   price of the robots

2. Who will probably answer the telephone at Advanced Technologies?

    a.   Mike Epstein
    b.   a receptionist
    c.   Epstein's secretary

3. When will Epstein and Blake probably meet?

    a.   today
    b.   tomorrow
    c.   next week

4. Where might Blake and Epstein meet?

    a.   Epstein's office
    b.   Blake's hotel
    c.   a restaurant

Now listen to the tape.

B. General Comprehension

Mark the sentences true (T) or false (F).

1. Mike Epstein is too busy to meet with Charles Blake.   T/F
2. They will meet tomorrow.   T/F
3. Epstein wants Blake to meet Shirley Graham.   T/F
4. Blake is busy on Wednesday and can't meet Ms. Graham.   T/F
5. Ms. Graham is Blake's secretary.   T/F

C. Detailed Listening

Listen to the tape again. Indicate the correct answer by circling a, b, or c.

1. Blake tells the receptionist
   a. he's in San Francisco.
   b. his full name and the name of his company.
   c. the time of the meeting.

2. Blake and Epstein will meet
   a. before 11:00 Tuesday.
   b. at 11:15 Tuesday.
   c. at 11:15 Wednesday.

3. They will meet at
   a. Epstein's office.
   b. a restaurant.
   c. Blake's hotel.

4. Epstein wants Blake to meet Graham because
   a. she is interested in Japan.
   b. she is the president of the company.
   c. she's in charge of the project that Epstein is working on.

5. The meeting on Wednesday
   a. is not finalized.
   b. is definite.
   c. is not possible.

D. Role Play

Work in groups of three. Take turns role-playing parts A, B, and C below. The situation is the same as above. Then listen to the tape again and go on to the next page.

Part A
Make an appointment to see C at Advanced Technologies. You are staying at the Hilton Hotel. You would like to see C as soon as possible. You work for Yamashita Ltd. Confirm the time and place of meeting.

Part B
You are the receptionist at Advanced Technologies.

Part C
You are expecting A's call. You want to meet A tomorrow, and you want A to meet with your boss, Shirley Graham, on Wednesday. Confirm the details of the meeting. Your office is near the Hilton Hotel.

E. Functional Phrases

Listen to the tape, line by line, and write the correct phrase from the list below.

1. Offering, Introducing, Requesting

    Receptionist: Advanced Technologies. _____

    Blake: Yes. _____ Charles Blake of Yamashita Limited.

    _____ Mike Epstein, please.

    Receptionist: Just a minute and I'll put you through.

I'd like to speak with . . .	This is . . .	May I help you?

2. Greeting, Requesting, Agreeing, Clarifying

    Epstein: Hello Mr. Blake.

    Blake: Hello Mr. Epstein. _____

    Epstein: _____ How are you?

    Blake: Great.

    Epstein: Uh, when did you get in to San Francisco?

    Blake: Well I just arrived at my hotel a few moments ago.

    Epstein: Oh, uh, well _____ get together?

    Blake: I was wondering _____

    arrange a meeting for tomorrow sometime.

    Epstein: _____ I'll be free after eleven o'clock.

    _____

    Blake: Ah, that sounds fine with me.

How's that?	Yes, that's fine.	if we could possibly * . . .
How are you?	I'm fine thanks.	when should we . . .

* Note: *'I was wondering if we could (possibly) . . .' can be interchanged with 'Could we . . .'.*

3. Getting Attention and Requesting

Epstein: Okay, _____ . . . uh, one of our,

_____ introduce you to one of our Vice-Presidents,

Ms. Shirley Graham. She's in charge of the project that I'm working on. Uh,

I was wondering _____ get together, uh, say on

Wednesday.

Blake: Ah-h, I have no plans on Wednesday, and I would like to meet her.

| if we could . . . | I'd like to . . . | one more thing . . . |

F. Supplementary Exercises

VARIATION 1:   Making an appointment

Read the telephone dialog below. Choose the best answer for each blank.
Then listen to the tape to check your answers.

Bliss: Webber Industries, may I help you?

Milton: Yes. _____

          a. This is Bob Milton.   b. This is Mr. Milton.

Bliss: This is Sam Bliss speaking. How are you Mr. Milton?

Milton: _____

          a. Fine and you?   b. How are you?

Bliss: Just fine, thank you.

Milton: I'm calling to see if we can arrange a meeting. There are several matters I'd like

          to discuss with you.

Bliss: Okay, when would be convenient?

Milton: _____

          a. I want to meet with you tomorrow.   b. Could we meet tomorrow?

Bliss: Yes, that's possible. What time would be convenient?

Milton: _____

          a. How about 2:30?   b. I'd like to see you at 2:30.

Bliss: Fine. I'm looking forward to seeing you.

Milton: Me too. Okay, in your office at 2:30 tomorrow, right?

Bliss: Right. See you then.

Milton: See you tomorrow.

VARIATION 2:   Leaving a message

Listen to the tape and write in the exact words.

Receptionist: Webber Industries, _____ ?

Milton: _____ from

                Myer's Shipping Company. _____

                _____ ?

Receptionist: _____ Mr. Webber is not here right now. Can I take a

                message?

Milton: Yes. Could you please ask Mr. Webber to call me back before 5:00 today?

Receptionist: Yes sir. _____

                _____ ?

Milton: Certainly. M - I - L - T - O - N.

Receptionist: _____

                _____ ?

Milton: Yes. 877-3088.

EPISODE 3

Confirming Plans

STORY UPDATE

It is now Tuesday, June 11th. It is four o'clock in the afternoon. Mr. Epstein, from Advanced Technologies, met with Mr. Blake, from Yamashita Ltd., earlier today. They had lunch together and talked about industrial robots. Mr. Blake wants to sell his company's industrial robots to Advanced Technologies, Mr. Epstein's company.

Mr. Epstein's boss is Ms. Shirley Graham. She is in charge of a large project to build a new factory. The new factory is scheduled for completion this October. Tomorrow she is going to meet with Mr. Epstein and Mr. Blake. Mr. Epstein needs to confirm the arrangements with her. He is now at her office.

Discussion Questions

1. What did Blake and Epstein talk about earlier today?

2. Who is Shirley Graham?

3. What is going to happen tomorrow?

25

> **Scene Description** It is now 4:00 p.m. on Tuesday, June 11th. Mike Epstein met with Charles Blake earlier today. Now Mr. Epstein is back at his office. He has just made reservations at a restaurant for tomorrow's meeting with Mr. Blake. In this scene he goes to Ms. Shirley Graham's office to confirm plans for tomorrow.

A. Pre-listening

1. Why does Epstein want to talk with Graham?

2. What questions are the most important for Epstein to confirm?
    (*Rank your choices from 1–3.*)
    a. Is she free for the meeting?
    b. What is the purpose of the meeting?
    c. When and where should they meet?

3. Mike Epstein probably _____ to buy industrial robots from Yamashita Ltd.
    (*Circle your choice.*)
    a. wants
    b. doesn't want

4. At tomorrow's meeting, Ms. Graham wants
    (*Rank your choices from 1–3.*)
    a. to learn more about Yamashita Ltd.
    b. to discuss problems.
    c. to get to know Mr. Blake.

5. Yamashita Ltd. has no experience in North America. As a result, what kind of problems might they have in selling their robots in the U.S.?
    (*Rank your choices from 1–3.*)
    a. high shipping costs
    b. providing service and spare parts
    c. advertizing and marketing

B. General Comprehension

Now listen to the tape.

1. Ms. Graham cannot meet Mr. Blake because she's too busy.   T/F
2. Ms. Graham wants to change the time of the meeting.   T/F
3. Epstein had a good meeting with Blake earlier today.   T/F
4. Epstein is against buying robots from Yamashita.   T/F
5. Graham thinks there are some problems.   T/F

C. Detailed Listening

Now listen to the tape once more and complete the following sentences.

1. Epstein and Graham will leave their office at _____ tomorrow.

    a. 11:45
    b. 12:00
    c. 12:15

2. Epstein is going to pick up Graham at

    a. her office.
    b. Blake's hotel.
    c. his office.

3. Graham is worried about the problem of

    a. high shipping costs.
    b. aftersales service and the October deadline.
    c. advertizing and marketing.

4. Mike Epstein thinks that

    a. there isn't a problem.
    b. Yamashita's technology is excellent.
    c. they should decide not to buy robots from Yamashita Ltd.

5. Graham says, 'Yes. All right. Let's discuss it further tomorrow.' In this conversation, this means:

    a. I agree. Let's discuss it further tomorrow.
    b. I don't agree and I don't want to discuss it further.
    c. I understand, but I don't want to discuss it now.

D. Role Play

Work in pairs. Take turns role-playing parts A and B below. The situation is the same as above. Then listen to the tape again and go on to the next page.

Part A
In this short meeting with your boss, B, confirm the details for tomorrow's meeting with Charles Blake. You are in favor of buying robots from Yamashita, and you hope B will agree.

Part B
You are worried about several problems with Yamashita. You and A are going to meet with Mr. Blake of Yamashita Ltd. tomorrow. You need to confirm the details of the meeting with A.

E. Functional Phrases

Listen to the tape, line by line. Write the correct phrase from the list at the end of the section.

1. Requesting, Offering, and Confirming

    Graham: Come in.

    Epstein: Oh, Shirley, _____

    Graham: Sure. Come on in Mike. _____

    Epstein: Oh, thanks. Listen, _____

    _____ that I've made reservations for lunch tomorrow

    afternoon around 12:15. Okay?

    Graham: With Mr. Blake?

    Epstein: _____ of Yamashita Limited.

    Graham: Okay. So, we should leave here at . . .

    Epstein: About 12:00.

    Graham: 12:00 _____

    Epstein: Okay, good. I'll pick you up here at 12:00 and we can go over to his hotel
    together.

. . . sounds just fine.	do you have a minute?	I just wanted to let you know . . .
That's right . . .	Have a seat.	

2. Disagreeing Politely, Giving an Opinion, and Stalling

    Epstein: Yes, I did, and again I was very impressed with his flexibility and his . . .

    _____ that we can work things out with him.

    Graham: Okay. As long as it's clear to both of you that it has to be worked out, and be-
    fore October, because that's our deadline.

    Epstein: Well, again, _____

    _____ Shirley, but again the technology of their product

    is really excellent. _____ we really have to go ahead with this.

    Graham: Yes. All right. Well, _____

_____ All right?

Epstein: Okay. All right. Thank you. We'll see you tomorrow.

. . . let's discuss it further tomorrow.   I understand your reservations . . .
I think . . .   I think . . .

F. Supplementary Exercises

VARIATION 1:   Checking an appointment

Here are two parts of a dialog. Read the part on the left (Mrs. Powers' part).
Now find the correct order for the part on the right (Mr. Malone's part).
After you have finished, listen to the tape and check your answer.

Powers   Malone

1. Excuse me. Do you have a minute?   a. How about 1:00 on Friday?
2. Thanks. I made an appointment for us to   b. Would you call him back and see if Fri-
    see Mr. Myers. Are you still free at 11:00   day is good for him?
    on Wednesday?   c. 11:00 on Wednesday? I'm afraid not.
3. That's too bad.   I'm busy all morning.
4. That's fine with me.   d. Thanks.
5. Sure. I'll call him right away.   e. Certainly. Please come in.

VARIATION 2:   Changing an appointment

Listen to the telephone conversation and answer the questions below.

1. Why can't they meet at 11:00 on Wednesday?
2. Why does Mr. Myers want to meet before Friday?
3. What is Mrs. Powers going to do later today?

G. Group Practice

Practice role-playing the variations. Use your real name, but take the position of the
characters in the story.

An Important Introduction

STORY UPDATE

It is now Wednesday, June 12th. Yesterday Mr. Charles Blake from Yamashita Ltd. and Mr. Mike Epstein from Advanced Technologies met for lunch. After their meeting, Mr. Epstein took Mr. Blake on a short tour of San Francisco.

Today, Mr. Blake is going to meet Ms. Graham. Ms. Graham is a Vice-President at Advanced Technologies. She is in charge of a large project to build a new factory. Mr. Blake wants to sell his company's industrial robots for use in the new factory. Ms. Graham is interested in Yamashita's robots. However, she is also worried about several problems, such as aftersales service, spare parts, and storage space. She is also worried about doing business with a foreign company such as Yamashita Ltd.

Discussion Questions

1. Why is Mr. Blake going to meet Ms. Graham?

2. What kind of problems is Ms. Graham worried about?

3. Why do you think Ms. Graham is worried about doing business with a foreign company?

Scene Description   Mike Epstein and Shirley Graham have arrived at the San Francisco Hilton Hotel and are looking for Charles Blake. They are scheduled to meet him and have lunch together.

A. Pre-listening

1. What are the relationships among Blake, Epstein, and Graham?
    Match the names with the correct description.

    Blake and Epstein   a.   They have never met.
    Graham and Epstein   b.   They are old friends.
    Graham and Blake   c.   They have met several times on business and
                                       have played golf together.
                                  d.   They work together in the same company.
                                       She is his boss.

2. *Circle the correct form/s of address in this situation.*

    Mike Epstein addresses Charles Blake as: Mr. Blake/Charles

    Mike Epstein addresses Shirley Graham as: Ms. Graham/Shirley

    Shirley Graham addresses Mike Epstein as: Mr. Epstein/Mike

    Shirley Graham addresses Charles Blake as: Mr. Blake/Charles

    Charles Blake addresses Shirley Graham as: Ms. Graham/Shirley

    Charles Blake addresses Mike Epstein as: Mr. Epstein/Mike

3. After introductions, the first thing they will discuss is
    (*Rank your choices from 1–3.*)

    a.   the weather.
    b.   business.
    c.   Mr. Blake's trip.

4. Who arranged this meeting?

5. Who is the most important person at this meeting?

Now listen to the tape.

B. General Comprehension

1. Mr. Epstein introduced Mr. Blake to Ms. Graham.   T/F
2. They discussed business right after the introductions. T/F
3. This is Blake's first trip to San Francisco.   T/F
4. They are going to have lunch together.   T/F
5. They are going to eat lunch in the hotel.   T/F

C. Detailed Listening

Now listen to the tape once more and complete the following sentences (for 2, answer the questions).

1. When Mike and Shirley arrived at the hotel Charles Blake was

    a. waiting in his hotel room.
    b. reading a newspaper in the lobby.
    c. talking with a friend.

2. How long ago was Blake in San Francisco?

    a. This is his first trip to San Francisco.
    b. He was in San Francisco seven years ago.
    c. He was in San Francisco for a brief visit.

3. Yesterday Charles Blake

    a. went to Fisherman's Wharf with an old friend.
    b. saw a bit of San Francisco with Mike Epstein.
    c. visited the West Coast for the first time.

4. Last time Blake was in San Francisco, he stayed

    a. for about the same length of time as this time.
    b. for only a day or two.
    c. for a week or longer.

5. Mike Epstein interrupts the conversation because

    a. they have a reservation at a restaurant.
    b. he wants to continue the conversation.
    c. they are going to walk to a restaurant.

D. Role Play

Work in groups of three. Take turns role-playing parts A, B, and C below. The situation is the same as above. Then listen to the tape again and go on to the next exercise.

Part A
You are in Blake's role. You had a good time with B yesterday, and you are looking forward to meeting C.

Part B
You are in Epstein's role. Introduce C to A, and act as the host. You have made reservations for lunch.

Part C
You are in Graham's role. Welcome A to San Francisco, and ask questions about A's trip.

E. Functional Phrases

Listen to the tape, line by line, and write the exact words.

1. Introducing and Greeting

    Blake: Oh, hi Mike. _____ today?

    Epstein: Oh, _____ Charles.

    _____ our Vice-President, Shirley Graham. Shirley,

    _____ Charles Blake from Yamashita Ltd.

    Graham: _____ Mr. Blake.

    Blake: _____ Ms. Graham.

    Graham: _____

    Blake: _____

    Graham: Just fine. Mike tells me that . . .

This is . . .	It's nice to meet you . . .	Pleased to meet you . . .	Fine. And you?
this is . . .	it's good to see you . . .	How are you today?	How are you . . .

2. Interrupting, Suggesting, Agreeing

    Epstein: Well, _____ but we have a car

outside and we have reservations at 12:15. So _____

get over to the restaurant and we can continue our conversation there.

Graham: Okay.

Epstein: Okay?

Blake and Epstein: Okay? _____ to me.

Epstein: Okay. _____

That sounds fine . . .	Let's go!	why don't we . . .	I hate to interrupt . . .

F. Supplementary Exercises

Listen to the variations and fill in the blanks.

VARIATION 1:   Introducing yourself

Bob Myers comes to the office of Delta Electronics. Mrs. Powers comes down to the reception area and introduces herself.

Read the dialog below. Choose the best answers for each blank. Then listen to the tape to check your answers.

Powers: Mr. Myers?

Myers: Yes. _____

        a. That's right.   b. And you?

Powers: _____ Sandra Powers. I work with Mr. Malone.

        a. I'm . . .   b. This is . . .

Myers.   Mrs. Powers. _____ I've been looking

forward to meeting you. (*They shake hands.*)

        a. How are you today?   b. How do you do?

Powers: _____ Mr. Myers. You've

come a very long way on this trip, so I hope things are going well. Welcome to

San Francisco!

        a. It's nice to meet you . . .   b. I'm doing fine . . .

VARIATION 2:   Looking for someone

Mr. Malone asks Mrs. Powers to meet Bob Myers at his hotel. They are taking him out to lunch in a restaurant. Mrs. Powers looks for Bob Myers.

Look at the following incomplete dialog. Imagine the complete dialog. Then listen to the tape and write in the exact words.

Powers: Mr. Myers?

X: _____ ?

Powers: _____ Mr. Myers from Dover Limited?

X: No, _____

_____ ask reception to page him?

Powers: Oh, thank you. I'll do that. _____ .

X: Oh, _____ .

G. Group Practice

Practice role-playing the original situation, Variation 1 and Variation 2.
In all cases use your real name, but take the position of the characters in the story.

Extra Practice

Work in groups and practice using the phrases below in different situations
(e.g. in your office, at a restaurant, in a meeting, etc.)

This is	Pleased to meet you.
It's nice to meet you.	Are you . . .
How do you do?	I'm . . .
How are you today?	Fine. And you?
It's good to see you.	
I hate to interrupt but . . .	
Sorry to bother you . . .	Not at all.

EPISODE 5

A Business Lunch

STORY UPDATE

It is now Wednesday, June 12th. It is 1:30 in the afternoon. Mr. Blake, Mr. Epstein, and Ms. Graham are having lunch together at a restaurant. Mr. Blake wants to sell his company's industrial robots to Advanced Technologies. Ms. Graham, of Advanced Technologies, is in charge of a large project to build a new electronics factory. In this factory they will need many industrial robots. Mr. Epstein thinks that the robots made by Yamashita Ltd. are the best. Ms. Graham agrees, but she is worried about several other problems. Mr. Blake needs to convince her that these problems can be solved.

Discussion Questions

1. Why are industrial robots important for the new factory?

2. What problems do you think are most important for Ms. Graham to consider?

Scene Description   Blake, Epstein and Graham are having lunch together at a restaurant. They are discussing the possibility of Advanced Technologies buying industrial robots from Yamashita Limited. Graham is worried about several important problems.

A. Pre-listening

1. Who do you think will be the host at the restaurant?
    (*Rank your choices from 1–3.*)

    a. Epstein
    b. Graham
    c. Blake

    Why do you think so?

2. Which of the following problems are most important to discuss at the meeting?
    (*Rank your choices from 1–4.*)

    a. spare parts and maintenance in the United States
    b. cost of the robots
    c. contract details
    d. shipping costs

3. What do you think is the most likely solution to the problem of maintenance and spare parts?
    (*Rank your choices from 1–4.*)

    a. Yamashita will open an office in the United States.
    b. Yamashita will ask Advanced Technologies to store extra spare parts.
    c. Yamashita will train Advanced Technologies' engineers.
    d. other (why?)

4. Do you think a final decision will be made at this meeting? Why?

Now listen to the tape.

B. General Comprehension

1. Nobody wants more coffee.   T/F
2. There are no major problems.   T/F
3. Graham needs more information.   T/F
4. Advanced Technologies will definitely buy the robots.   T/F
5. Graham is worried about doing business with a Japanese company.   T/F

C. Detailed Listening

Now listen to the tape once more and complete the sentences below.

1. _____ would like another cup of coffee.

    a. Epstein
    b. Graham
    c. Blake

2. Graham and Blake agree that the basic problem is that Yamashita doesn't have

    _____ or

    _____ in the United States.

3. Blake's first proposal was that

    a. Yamashita open an office in the United States.
    b. Advanced Technologies use their warehouse to store spare parts.
    c. Advanced Technologies take care of maintenance.

4. Graham needs to know a lot more detail before she can make a decision about Blake's

    proposal. Warehouse space is limited, so she needs to know the _____

    and the _____ of the spare parts.

5. Another reason Graham may decide not to buy from Yamashita is that Advanced Tech-

    nologies has never _____ with a Japanese company before.

D. Role Play

Work in groups of three. Take turns role-playing parts A, B, and C below. The situation is the same as above. Then listen to the tape again and go on to the next page.

Part A
You are in Blake's role. You want to confirm your understanding of all the points made by C. Then make a proposal.

Part B
You are in Epstein's role. You want A and C to understand each other. You are the host. Make sure everyone is comfortable.

Part C
You are in Graham's role. You are worried about several problems. Explain these problems to A.

E. Functional Phrases

Listen to the tape, line by line, and write the exact words.

1. Offering, Declining, and Requesting

    Epstein: Well, that was a pretty good meal.

    Graham: Um, it was delicious.

    Epstein: ＿＿＿＿＿＿＿＿＿＿＿＿＿＿＿＿＿ some . . . some more coffee?
    Shirley?

    Graham: ＿＿＿＿＿＿＿＿＿＿ No thank you.

    Blake: Yes. ＿＿＿＿＿＿＿＿＿ a little bit more please.

    Epstein: Okay. There's the waiter. Waiter, ＿＿＿＿＿＿＿＿ have another cup
    of coffee over here please. Thank you.

Not for me.	I'd like . . .	Would anyone like . . .	could we . . .

---

2. Confirming, Agreeing, Promising, Clarifying/Qualifying

    Blake: Okay. Ms. Graham, ＿＿＿＿＿＿＿＿＿＿＿＿＿＿＿＿＿＿＿＿
    ＿＿＿＿＿＿＿＿＿＿ correctly on this. Now, your basic problem is that
    we at Yamashita can not provide adequate maintenance or spare parts
    quickly enough.

    Graham: Yes. ＿＿＿＿＿＿＿＿＿＿＿＿＿ That's my main concern.

    Blake: Okay. Now you've rejected the proposal that we use your warehouse for
    storage space for spare parts.

    Graham: Well, ＿＿＿＿＿＿＿＿＿＿＿＿＿ Mr. Blake.
    ＿＿＿＿＿＿＿＿＿＿＿＿＿＿＿ that a little. Space is limited and it
    would depend very much on the quantity of parts, the size etcetera.
    ＿＿＿＿＿＿＿＿＿＿＿ need a lot more detail on that.

    Blake: I can certainly understand your concerns. I'm going to put this information in
    a report after I telex Tokyo.

    Graham: Okay.

Blake: And _____ the report ready for you tomorrow. And

maybe we can come up with a solution to the problem.

Graham: Okay. Well, that sounds fine. _____ Mr. Blake, I can't

make any guarantees. You know we've never done business with a Japanese

company before so it's quite an undertaking.

I would . . .   not entirely . . .   I'll have . . .   That's right . . .
Even then . . .   let me see if I understand you . . .   Let me clarify . . .

F. Supplementary Exercises

VARIATION: Negotiating

General Comprehension Questions

Mr. Davis and Mr. Jones are at the end of a meeting. Several problems have already been discussed.
Listen to the variation on the tape and answer the questions below.

1.   How many problems are there? What are they?
2.   Which problem is the most difficult? Why?
3.   What does Davis promise to do?

Functional Phrases

Now read the variation dialog below. Imagine the complete dialog. Then look at the list of phrases.
Choose the best answer for each blank. Then listen to the tape again to check your answers.

Davis: _____ there are still problems with the delivery date

and the size of the discount, but _____ is okay,

is that right?

Jones: Yes. _____ The price is higher than we expected, and

we need delivery within six months at the latest.

Davis: I see. Well, _____ The

delivery date is going to be a problem, but _____ and see

if it's possible. _____ again?

_____ later this week?

Jones: Okay, but ——————————— I won't be free ————————————

tomorrow afternoon. ——————————————

Davis: No, that'll be fine. How about 3:00?

Jones: Okay, good. I'll see you tomorrow, Mr. Davis.

Davis: See you then.

I'm afraid . . .	How about . . .	except for . . .	everything else . . .
Is that too early?	To summarize, . . .	Can we get together . . .	
I'll see what I can do.	I'll check . . .	That's right.	

G. Group Practice

Practice role-playing the variation.

The Disagreement

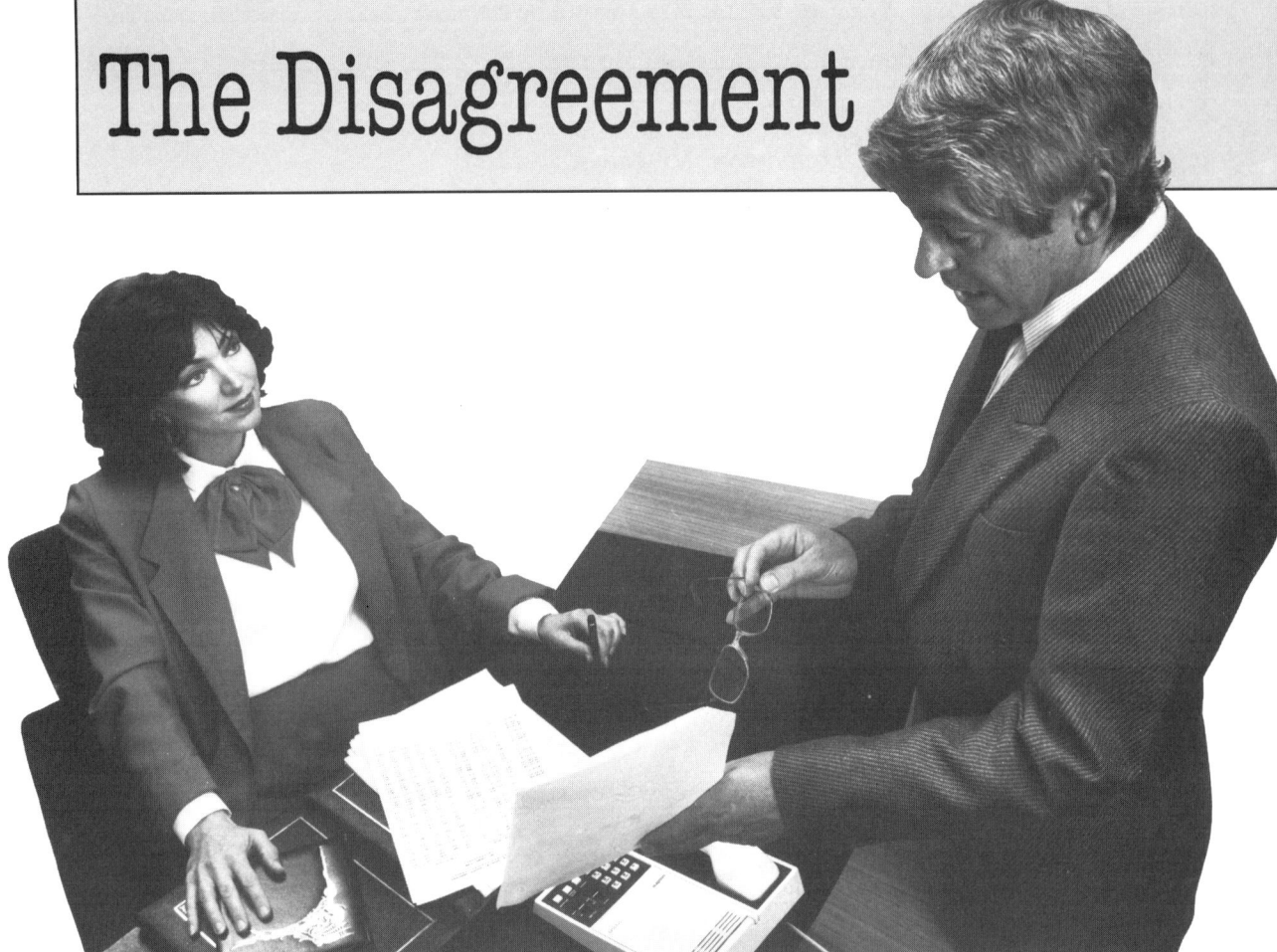

STORY UPDATE

It is now Wednesday afternoon, June 12th. Mr. Epstein and Ms. Graham have finished their meeting with Mr. Blake. They are now in Ms. Graham's office. They are discussing their meeting with Mr. Blake.

Ms. Graham is worried about doing business with Yamashita. She thinks it would be safer to buy robots from an American company, United Industries. Spare parts and maintenance wouldn't be a problem because the United Industries factory is close, and in the past they have always been reliable. Their technological level, however, is not as high as Yamashita's, and their price is a bit higher.

Discussion Questions

1. What is Epstein's job?

2. What is Graham's job?

3. What are reasons for and against buying from United Industries?

Scene Description Mike Epstein and Shirley Graham are meeting in her office. They are discussing the reasons for and against buying robots from Yamashita Limited.

A. Pre-listening

1. What is the deadline for installing the robots in the new factory? Why is this a problem?
2. If Epstein and Graham don't agree, who will make the decision?
3. Below are the notes Graham made during the luncheon meeting with Blake.

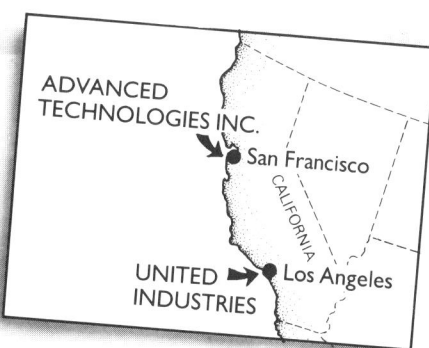

Shirley Graham Vice-President

Wed, June 12ᵗʰ
YAMASHITA LTD - BLAKE

Advantages

- Price
- State-of-the-Art Technology
- Excellent maintenance record in Japan

NOTE: United Industries has been a reliable supplier for 15 years.

Disadvantages

- Deadline ??
- No experience in the U.S.
- We have never worked with this company.

What do you think Graham will decide?   *Now listen to the tape.*

B. General Comprehension

1. Graham wants to buy the robots from United Industries.	T/F
2. Graham is worried about Yamashita's reliability.	T/F
3. Epstein agrees with Graham.	T/F
4. Graham doesn't want to take a risk with Yamashita.	T/F
5. Graham thinks Epstein hasn't done a good job.	T/F

C. Detailed Listening

Now listen to the tape once more and complete the following sentences.

1. Graham is afraid that

    a. Yamashita's technology is not reliable.
    b. Yamashita cannot be relied on to install the robots on time.
    c. the quality of Yamashita's robots isn't good enough.

2. Graham wants to buy from United Industries because

    a. their robots are less expensive.
    b. she is sure they can install the robots on time.
    c. their technology is just as good as Yamashita's.

3. Epstein says that it is good that Yamashita isn't established in North America, because

    a. his company can get Yamashita's technology first.
    b. Yamashita will design an excellent support system.
    c. Yamashita will discount the price.

4. For Epstein, the main reason to buy from Yamashita is

    a. that the deadline isn't a problem.
    b. that United Industries' robots are too expensive.
    c. that Yamashita's technology is the best.

5. Graham says, 'I'm sorry, but I'm afraid on this you're just not going to be able to have it the way you want it.' In this conversation, this means

    a. Graham is afraid of Epstein.
    b. she disagrees with Epstein's recommendation.
    c. she is right and he is wrong.

D. Role Play

Work in pairs. Take turns role-playing parts A and B below. The situation is the same as above. Then listen to the tape again and go on to the next page.

Part A
You are in Epstein's role. Try to persuade B that Advanced Technologies should buy robots from Yamashita.

Part B
You are in Graham's role. Explain your reasons for not buying robots from Yamashita. Explain the reasons for buying from United Industries.

E. Functional Phrases

Listen to the tape line by line, and write the exact words.

1. Giving an Opinion and Disagreeing

    Graham: . . . Yes, in Japan. The quality of their product is extremely good but I don't
    know anything about their reliability. Can they be relied on to do this by Octo-
    ber 1st? _____ we've worked with United Industries before
    and _____ just go ahead on the
    deal with them. _____ that they can have every-
    thing installed and working by October 1st.

    Epstein: Well, look, _____
    Shirley, and that is that _____
    they haven't established themselves in the States _____ that's
    an advantage . . . . that's our advantage because we can get their technology
    before other companies can. If we're willing to take the risk.
    _____ take that risk.

I think we should . . .	I think we really have to . . .	I agree with you. . . . but . . .
I feel sure . . .	but there's another argument . . .	You know . . .

2. Disagreeing, Giving an Opinion, Complimenting

    Graham: Well, _____ that's basically what it comes down to Mike. You
    want to take the risk and I really am not willing to. _____
    that I can afford to take the risk.

    Epstein: Oh, but what have I been doing for the last year? I've been looking for the new
    technology to really make this factory something special and I think that this is
    what we need to do. _____ you
    disagree with this. It's very clear.

    Graham: And I think _____ but
    _____ that there are more disadvantages than advantages.

And ———————————————————————————————————

on this you're just not going to be able to have it the way you want it.

I'm sorry but I'm afraid . . .	I think . . .	you've done a very good job . . .
I can't understand why . . .	I don't feel . . .	I think . . .

Note: *From here on in the text, phrases are not given.*
  Good luck!

F. Supplementary Exercises

VARIATION: Making a choice

Here are two parts of a dialog. Read the part on the left (Mr. Malone's part). Now find the correct order for the part on the right (Mrs. Powers' part). After you have finished, listen to the tape and check your answers.

Malone

1. I think we should hire John Hart. He has ten years of experience and he's 35 years old, quite mature. What do you think?

2. Yes, he does have an M.B.A. degree, but he doesn't have any real job experience.

3. Yes, that's a good point. Maybe we need more information. Let's talk with them both again.

4. Well, I agree, time is a problem. But this new position is very important. We can wait one more day. Would you mind calling them back?

Powers

a. Do you really think that's necessary? A second interview is a good idea, but I don't think we have the time. I think we really have to decide today.

b. I don't agree. I think we should hire Kevin Ward. He's much better educated, and very bright.

c. That's true, but Mr. Hart has only four years' experience in sales.

d. All right. I'll try to schedule them both for tomorrow afternoon.

Listen to the tape again, and answer the questions below.

1. What are the qualifications of Kevin Ward and John Hart?
2. What is Mrs. Powers' opinion?
3. What is Mr. Malone's opinion?

G. Group Practice

Practice role-playing the variation.

EPISODE 7

Keeping in Touch

STORY UPDATE

It is Thursday afternoon, June 13th. Mr. Epstein and Mr. Blake are in Epstein's office. They have just finished meeting with Ms. Graham. At that meeting, Blake gave a report to Ms. Graham with a proposal to further discount the price of the robots. In addition, Yamashita would send two engineers to Advanced Technologies. They would provide training in how to service the robots. A large number of spare parts, however, would have to be stored by Advanced Technologies. Ms. Graham was pleased with Blake's report, but she decided not to buy the robots from Yamashita.

Mr. Epstein disagrees with Graham's decision, and he is thinking about resigning. He feels that Advanced Technologies will not succeed if it is not willing to take risks. He thinks it is a mistake not to have the very best technology in the new factory. He hopes to keep in touch with Mr. Blake for future possibilities.

Discussion Questions

1. Do you think Graham's decision was a good decision? Why?

2. Do you think Graham is a good manager? Why?

3. What do you think of Epstein?

> **Scene Description** It is now 1:30 p.m. on Friday. The final meeting between Blake, Epstein and Graham has just finished, and Blake and Epstein are in Epstein's office. Blake has made plans to fly to New York tomorrow. Another company, Federal Motors, is interested in Yamashita's robots and he is scheduled to meet with them on Monday.

A. Pre-listening

1. What will Blake's reaction be to Graham's decision?
    a.   He will be surprised.
    b.   He will not be surprised.
    Why?

2. Epstein is not happy with the decision.
    a.   He will not tell Blake his opinion.
    b.   He will tell Blake his opinion.
    Why do you think so?

3. In this business situation, Blake and Epstein should
    a.   arrange to stay in touch.
    b.   not arrange to stay in touch.
    Why?

Now listen to the tape.

B. General Comprehension

1. Blake is surprised by the decision not to buy from Yamashita.   T/F
2. Epstein tells Blake he isn't happy with the decision.   T/F
3. Blake is going to return to Japan immediately.   T/F
4. Epstein invited Blake to play golf with him.   T/F
5. Blake is busy, so he can't accept Epstein's invitation.   T/F

C. Detailed Listening

Now listen to the tape once more and complete the following sentences.

1. Blake says this is a valuable experience because
    a.   their robots aren't good enough for the North American market.
    b.   he is under a lot of pressure.
    c.   now he knows what their biggest problem will be.

2. Epstein says that they couldn't convince Graham to buy from Yamashita because
   a. Graham didn't like the quality of the robots.
   b. she was under a lot of time pressure.
   c. she was incompetent.

3. Tomorrow afternoon Blake is flying to New York to
   a. visit friends.
   b. meet with prospective customers.
   c. look for a new job.

4. Epstein wants to stay in touch because
   a. he is interested in Yamashita's robots for possible future projects.
   b. he enjoys playing golf with Blake.
   c. Shirley Graham is going to be fired and he will take over.

5. Epstein has made reservations
   a. at a restaurant.
   b. to play golf at his club.
   c. to fly to New York.

D. Role Play

Work in pairs. Take turns role-playing parts A and B below. The situation is the same as above. Then listen to the tape again and go on to the next page.

Part A
You are in Epstein's role. Tell B that your company has decided not to buy robots from Yamashita. Try to keep a good relationship with B, and invite B to join you in a game of golf.

Part B
You are in Blake's role. Explain why you think Graham decided not to buy from you. Try to keep a good relationship with A. You are going to fly to New York tomorrow.

E. Functional Phrases

Listen to the tape, line by line, and write the exact words.

1. Expressing Disappointment, Giving an Opinion and Qualifying

   Epstein: Well, _____ but _____ things

   worked out the way we thought they might.

Blake: Yeah, but this has been a valuable experience for us. Now we know what our biggest problem will be with the North American market.

Epstein: Well _____ , of course, I'm still not happy. _____ that your machinery is the best on the market.

_____ that I . . . we couldn't convince Shirley. _____ , I can understand her point too. She's under a lot of pressure here to get this . . . this new operation going by O·tober.

Blake: Sure.

2. Requesting, Promising, Inviting, and Accepting

Epstein: Also, _____ , _____

_____ keep in touch later. I'm very interested to know what happens. In the future, you know, we never know what's going to happen but

_____ for us to work together.

Blake: Okay, _____ Mike.

Epstein: One other thing. _____ this afternoon?

Blake: Well, I have no plans.

Epstein: Well, I remember the nice game of golf that we had together when I was in Tokyo. I have a membership in a golf club just across the Bay here and I've made some reservations. _____

in a round of golf this afternoon?

Blake: _____ Sure.

F. Supplementary Exercises

VARIATION: Making a polite refusal

Ms. Cinthia Winthrop and Mr. Robert Vale have just finished a business meeting. Ms. Winthrop is an aggressive saleswoman for a New York company. Mr. Vale is on a business trip from London, and he is not interested in doing business with her.

Listen to the tape and answer the following questions.

1. What does Ms. Winthrop invite Mr. Vale to do?
2. How does Mr. Vale refuse both invitations?
3. Do you think they will keep in touch? Why?

Now listen to the tape again. Then look at the dialog below and **fill in the blanks using the phrases from the list below**. *Note that the phrases in the list below are different from the ones on the tape. Choose the phrase which has the closest meaning to what you hear on the tape.*

Winthrop: _____ to see our factory while you are in New York. I think you will find it quite interesting and . . .

Vale: That's very kind of you. _____ my schedule is booked up all next week. I'm meeting with several different companies while I'm here.

Winthrop: _____ Well _____ _____ I may be in London early next year and . . .

Vale: Please give me a ring then.

Winthrop: Thank you. _____ Well, it's nearly 12:30. _____ for lunch?

Vale: _____ I have other plans for this afternoon. _____

Winthrop: _____ Perhaps another time.

That's too bad.	I'm sorry but . . .	Let's keep in touch.
Why don't you join me. . . .	I'll do that.	Thank you anyway.
Not at all.	But I'm afraid . . .	I'd like to invite you . . .

G. Group Practice

Practice role-playing the variation.

EPISODE 8

New Customer

STORY UPDATE

It is Monday, June 17th. Mr. Blake has left San Francisco and is now in New York. He is scheduled to meet with Mr. Stewart Chapman of Federal Motors this morning. Mr. Chapman is a systems engineer and is a Vice-President at Federal Motors.

Federal Motors is an automobile company. It is a very large company, and it is now modernizing its present factories. Mr. Chapman is very interested in Yamashita's robots, and he has studied the technical information that was sent to him from Yamashita. He is impressed by Yamashita's high technology, and he is looking forward to meeting with Mr. Blake.

Discussion Questions

1. Who is Mr. Chapman?

2. Why is Federal Motors interested in Yamashita's robots?

Scene Description Mr. Blake has just arrived at the Federal Motors building in New York City. He has an appointment with Mr. Stewart Chapman to discuss the possibility of selling industrial robots to Federal Motors.

A. Pre-listening

1. According to the following letter, when is Mr. Blake scheduled to meet Mr. Chapman?

```
Stewart R. Chapman
Vice-President, Engineering
Federal Motors Building
New York, NY 10016
U.S.A.

Dear Mr. Chapman

Thank you for your letter of May 20th.  I am looking forward to
meeting you, and am pleased that you can meet with me the week of
June 17 while I am in New York.  I will call your office on Friday
morning, June 14 to confirm the exact time and details.

As you requested, I have enclosed the latest information on our
industrial robots.  I am confident that our robots will meet your
highest standards, and I look forward to discussing the details.
If things work out, I hope to meet you here in Tokyo in the not too
distant future.

Sincerely,

Charles Blake

Charles Blake
Manager, International Sales
```

2. In the above letter, a business meeting is being arranged. In your opinion, what are good reasons for changing or breaking a business appointment?
   (*Rank your choices from 1–5.*)

   a. a busy schedule with more important matters/clients
   b. personal matters (e.g. illness, family problems, etc.)

    c.   transportation/weather difficulties
    d.   forgetting the appointment
    e.   other (give examples)
          Why?

Now listen to the tape.

B. General Comprehension

1.   Dave Gomez and Charles Blake have met before.   T/F
2.   Gomez apologizes to Blake.   T/F
3.   Mr. Chapman is busy, so they have to wait.   T/F
4.   Blake will meet with Gomez instead of Chapman.   T/F
5.   Mr. Gomez wants to talk business immediately.   T/F

C. Detailed Listening

Now listen to the tape once more and complete the following sentences.

1.   Blake has an appointment with
      a.   Mr. Chapman later this week.
      b.   Mr. Chapman at 10:30.
      c.   Mr. Gomez at 10:30.

2.   Mr. Gomez explains that Mr. Chapman
      a.   is out of town on company business.
      b.   has quit working for Federal Motors.
      c.   is out of town on a personal matter.

3.   Mr. Chapman will
      a.   meet with Blake as soon as he returns.
      b.   not be involved in the negotiations.
      c.   be out of town for several weeks.

4.   Mr. Gomez knows about
      a.   Yamashita, but not its products.
      b.   Yamashita and its products.
      c.   industrial robots, but not Yamashita.

5.   Mr. Gomez suggests that they
      a.   wait for Chapman to return.
      b.   get to know each other a bit before discussing business.
      c.   reschedule the meeting for later this afternoon.

D. Role Play

Work in groups of three. Take turns role-playing parts A, B, and C below. The situation is the same as above. Then listen to the tape again and go on to the next exercise.

Part A
You are in Gomez's role. Explain why Mr. Chapman is absent and introduce yourself to C. Make C feel comfortable. Explain that you will act in Chapman's place.

Part B
You are the receptionist at Federal Motors.

Part C
You are in Blake's role. You have an appointment with Mr. Stewart Chapman. Find out why Mr. Chapman is absent.

E. Functional Phrases

Listen to the tape, line by line, and write the exact words.

1. Introducing

    Receptionist: Good morning sir, _____ ?

    Blake: Yeah, _____

    to see Mr. Chapman, Stewart Chapman at 10:30.

    Receptionist: Oh, Mr. Chapman. _____

    _____ ?

    Blake: Yeah, _____ is, uh, Blake, Charles Blake of

    Yamashita Limited.

    Receptionist: All right, thank you. Just a moment please . . .

2. Accepting, Apologizing, Requesting, Suggesting, Introducing

    Gomez: Good morning Mr. Blake. _____ Federal Motors. My

    name is Dave Gomez.

    Blake: _____ Mr. Gomez.

    Gomez: _____ sir. Did you have a

    good trip to New York?

    Blake: Yeah, and I'm looking forward to staying here for a few days and doing some

    business.

Gomez: Great. Uh, Mr. Chapman _____

_____ . He was called out of town on

a personal matter very suddenly. . . . In the meantime I'm quite familiar with

Yamashita and uh your products and uh, so _____

work with you _____ .

Blake: Okay, sure. And _____ about Mr. Chapman's

absence. _____ .

Gomez: Okay, great. Uh, well you must be tired from your trip, so _____

_____ go into the office and sit down and relax for a few minutes

and we can get some coffee or tea _____ ?

Blake: Okay, that sounds great.

Gomez: Great.

F. Supplementary Exercises

VARIATIONS: Asking a favor

Sandra Powers calls Bill Malone at home on Sunday. Listen to Variation I. You will hear only Sandra Powers' side of the conversation. Imagine the complete conversation. Then write in what you think Bill Malone says in the blanks below.

VARIATION 1

Malone: _____ .

Powers: Hello Bill. Sorry to call you at home.

Malone: _____ ?

Powers: I'm afraid I've got a problem. My mother is quite ill and I have to fly to Miami today.

I hate to ask, but would you mind meeting Bob Myers of Dover Limited, tomorrow?

Malone: _____

_____

_____ ?

Powers: He'll be there at 10:30.

Malone: _____ .

Powers: Thanks. Again, I'd like to apologize for this inconvenience.

Malone: _____

_____

_____ .

Powers: Thank you. I hope I can be back by Wednesday, but I'm just not sure right now.

Malone: _____ .

Powers: Thanks again. I appreciate it. I'll call you tomorrow afternoon around 4:00.

Malone: _____ .

VARIATION 2

In this variation, you will hear both sides of the conversation.
Compare what you wrote in Variation 1 with what Malone says in Variation 2.

G. Group Practice

Practice role-playing the variation.

EPISODE 9

Negotiations

STORY UPDATE

It is now Tuesday, June 18th. Mr. Chapman is still out of town and won't be back until tomorrow, so Mr. Blake is meeting with Dave Gomez. Yesterday they discussed the technology of the robots, the price, and a little about how the robots are being used by other companies in Japan. In general, Mr. Gomez was very impressed.

There are still several problems that need to be discussed. Mr. Blake is worried, because some of these problems are the same problems that forced Advanced Technologies to decide not to buy from Yamashita. On the other hand, one point in his favor is that there isn't as much time pressure as before. Federal Motors won't need the robots for about six months.

Discussion Questions

1. What new problems do you think might be discussed?

2. What kind of language problems do you think might be important to discuss?

58

> **Scene Description** It is now Tuesday, June 18th. Mr. Blake and Mr. Gomez have been talking for about an hour and a half. They are now reviewing several important points in the negotiations.

A. Pre-listening

1. What do you think are Yamashita's main strengths?
    (*Rank your choices from 1–4.*)

    a. aftersales service
    b. price
    c. quality and high performance
    d. good reputation

2. What are some important differences between international sales/service and domestic sales/service for a product such as industrial robots? Which of these differences are problems that are often difficult to solve?

3. How much time is usually necessary to solve these kinds of problems for an important new customer?
    (*Rank your choices from 1–4.*)

    a. six weeks or less
    b. three months
    c. six months
    d. approximately one year

Now listen to the tape.

B. General Comprehension

1. Time pressure is a major problem.   T/F
2. Yamashita has already translated the service manual into English.   T/F
3. Gomez needs more information about Yamashita's performance record in Japan.   T/F
4. Gomez isn't satisfied with Blake's answers.   T/F
5. From Blake's point of view, this meeting is successful.   T/F

C. Detailed Listening

Listen to the tape again. Indicate the correct answer by circling a, b, or c.

1. Gomez needs a group of technical advisors
    a. to translate the service manual into English.

b.   to train his engineers and workers.

c.   to provide language training

2.   The technical advisors can come to Federal Motors from Japan
a.   as soon as they learn to speak English.
b.   within a few months.
c.   anytime they are needed.

3.   Blake says the service manual will be ready
a.   in two weeks at the most.
b.   in a short time, but he's got to check.
c.   in several months.

4.   Gomez needs the service manual in English
a.   in two to three weeks.
b.   in a month or two.
c.   anytime before January 1st.

5.   Blake will send performance reports of the robots to Gomez
a.   early next year.
b.   as soon as they are finished.
c.   shortly after he gets back to Tokyo.

D. Role Play

Work in pairs. Take turns role-playing parts A and B below. The situation is the same as above. Then listen to the tape again and go on to the next exercise.

Part A
You are in Gomez's role. Summarize all problem areas and confirm your understanding of B's proposals.

Part B
You are in Blake's role. Confirm your understanding of all problem areas and propose solutions.

E. Functional Phrases

Listen to the tape, line by line, and write the exact words.

1.   Clarifying, Requesting, and Stalling

Gomez: . . . Uh when we first put these machines in operation, install them in our factories, can you send over a group of technical advisors who speak English and could train our engineers and workmen?

Blake: Certainly. _____ we have some engineers in a language training program now and they could come over within a few months and be available any time you need them.

Gomez: Great, great, that sounds good. Another one of our major concerns is the service
manual. We're quite concerned about getting a service manual in English that
will be easy to read and very clear and useful for our engineers.

Blake: Yeah. Again, _____ we are preparing a trans-
lation of the Japanese manual we have now, and we expect that to be ready in a
short time.

Gomez: _____ short time . . . _____ an
estimate?

Blake: Uh, _____ two weeks, _____
_____, _____ but probably
about two or three weeks.

Gomez: Oh, that sounds _____ .
_____ we have until January 1st to actually install
these machines and get them operating, so we're under no deadline pressure
here.

2. Accepting, Offering, Requesting, Promising/Assuring, Confirming

Blake: _____ send you some reports that we have on the
performance of the robot in some Japanese companies who are also our clients.
And _____ you'll be quite pleased with what you see.

Gomez: Okay, great. _____ get those off to me within a few weeks?

Blake: Sure. _____ .
_____ as soon as I get back to Tokyo _____ .

Gomez: Excellent. Thank you very much.

Blake: _____ .

Gomez: Well, no. That covers all the major points.

Blake: Okay. Fine.

Gomez: Sounds good . . .

F. Supplementary Exercises

VARIATIONS: Telling someone there have been changes

Business stories, like other stories, have different endings.

VARIATION 1

Bob Myers receives a telephone call in his hotel room on Wednesday afternoon.
Listen to the dialog once, and answer the following questions.

1.   What happened to Bill Malone?
2.   Why is Sandra Powers calling?
3.   Why isn't Myers' office in Tokyo open?

Now listen to the dialog again, and write in the exact words.

	Myers	Powers
1.	_____ _____	Bob? This is Sandra Powers.
2.	_____	Well that's why I'm calling you. There have been a few changes here, and I wanted to let you know.
3.	_____	Well, Bill Malone has resigned, and I've been put in charge of our project.
4.	_____ _____ _____	Thank you. But that's not all. I'm still interested in getting your machines for our new factory, and I've been able to extend the deadline a month, to November 1st. Do you think you can make it?
5.	_____ _____ _____	When are you flying back to Tokyo?
6.	_____	_____ change your flight and stop by here for a day or two?
7.	_____ _____ _____	Good. _____ call me back within a couple of hours and let me know, _____ .

FUNCTIONING IN BUSINESS
Answer Key

Note: The Key gives answers to the General Comprehension (B) and Detailed Listening (C) Sections of the text, together with transcripts of the dialogs on the cassette tape. The answers to Sections B and C, and the functional phrases used in the dialogs, are printed in bold type.

INTRODUCTION

Yamashita Ltd.

Yamashita Limited is a Japanese company. Its head office is in Tokyo, Japan. It manufactures industrial equipment and industrial robots. At this time 100 per cent of its sales of industrial robots are in Japan.

Comprehension
1. F   2. F

Advanced Technologies

Advanced Technologies is an American company. Its head office is in San Francisco, California. It manufactures electronic components and office computers. Eighty per cent of its sales are in the U.S., and twenty per cent overseas and in Canada.

Comprehension
1. T   2. F

Charles Blake

Mr. Blake graduated from Columbia University in 1971. He studied international relations, and also a little Japanese. Just after graduation he joined a small import–export company in New York. He worked as a salesman there for about five years. Then, in 1976, he joined Yamashita, a Japanese company. He is now working at Yamashita's head office in Tokyo. His main responsibility is to begin to export the company's industrial robots to North America. Mr. Blake lives in Tokyo and is married to a Japanese woman. He and his wife have one child, a son. He enjoys playing golf and tennis.

Comprehension
1. F   2. F   3. T   4. T

Mike Epstein

Mr. Epstein is a graduate of Stanford University, where he studied electrical engineering. After graduating in 1973, he worked for a small company in San Francisco for two years. He then went back to school in 1976 and got an M.B.A. In 1978 he was hired by Advanced Technologies. He is now a systems engineer, and he is responsible for cutting production costs for a new factory which is going to be built near San Francisco. He wants to increase the use of industrial robots in the factory to help cut costs and to improve productivity.
Mr. Epstein is divorced and has no children. He enjoys playing golf.

Comprehension
1. T   2. T   3. F   4. F

The Story

Two months ago, in April, Mike Epstein of Advanced Technologies went to Tokyo, Japan. He attended a trade show and saw many industrial robots. At the trade show he was very interested in the industrial robots made by Yamashita Limited. He met Charles Blake of Yamashita Limited and they talked about Yamashita's robots. After the trade show, Mr. Epstein and Mr. Blake played golf together. Then Mr. Epstein returned to the U.S.

Last month, in May, Mr. Blake of Yamashita Ltd., wrote a letter to Mr. Epstein. He said he would be in the U.S. in June, from June 10th through June 20th. If possible, he wanted to meet with Mr. Epstein.

Mr. Epstein wrote back and invited him to come to Advanced Technologies in San Francisco. Mr. Epstein wants to meet with Mr. Blake several times between June 11th and June 14th. Mr. Epstein is very interested in buying Yamashita's robots.

Comprehension

1. F   2. T   3. T

EPISODE 1: Checking In

B. General Comprehension

1. T   2. F   3. F   4. F   5. F

C. Detailed Listening

1. 14689   2. 10th; Thursday; 13th   3. $95   4. American Express card   5. One extra/one more/Friday; booked up/fully booked

E. Functional Phrases/Transcript

Clerk:	Good evening sir. Welcome to the San Francisco Hilton. **Can I help you?**
Blake:	Yeah, my name is Blake, Charles Blake. I have a confirmed reservation.
Clerk:	Mr. Blake, yes. What's the reservation number?
Blake:	Uh, let's see, 14689.
Clerk:	14689, let me check. Yes sir, we have your reservation right here. That's for June 10th through the 13th, Monday through Thursday night. **Is that correct**, sir?
Blake:	**Yes, that's fine.**
Clerk:	Okay, and the room sir is 685 on the sixth floor. I've got the key right here and I'll get a bellman for you (to) take you to your room.
Blake:	Okay. How much was the price of that room again?
Clerk:	That room is $95 a night, sir.
Blake:	Okay, fine. **Can I** use my American Express card for that?
Clerk:	**Yes, certainly** sir. Uh, **can I** do a print of your card before we check you in here?

Blake: Sure, here you are.
Clerk: Okay, thank you sir. All right, fine. We're all set here Mr. Blake, and I'll get the
            bellman right away. We'll get you to your room.
Blake: Oh, by the way, there's a chance that I will be staying one more day, uh, so I might
            be leaving on Saturday. **Is that okay?**
Clerk: Uh, let me check. Well sir, **I'm afraid** we're all booked up for Friday night, but
            something may open up. I can let you know.
Blake: Okay, **if you could** let me know as soon as possible, **I would appreciate it.**
Clerk: Yes, sir, **we'll** do that for you. Here's your key, sir. Bellman, front!

F. Supplementary Exercises

Variation

General Comprehension Questions

1. **Yes**   2. **No**   3. **No**   4. **Yes**

Functional Phrases/Transcript

Bank Teller: **May I help you?**
Customer: Yes. **Can I** change British pounds for American dollars here?
Bank Teller: Yes, certainly sir. How much would you like to change?
Customer: One hundred pounds please. Also, **could I** cash a personal check from my
               London Bank?
Bank Teller: **I'm afraid** that isn't possible. Our policy is that we do not cash out of town
               checks.
Customer: It's very important that I cash this check . . .
Bank Teller: Yes, I understand, but the bank policy . . .
Customer: **Could I** see the manager please?
Bank Teller: **I'm sorry but** the manager, Mr. Grover, is out right now. The assistant
               manager, Ms. Grace is in. Would that be all right?
Customer: **Yes. That's fine.** Thank you.
Bank Teller: Certainly. One moment please.

EPISODE 2:   Making an Appointment

B. General Comprehension

1. F   2. T   3. T   4. F   5. F

C. Detailed Listening

1. b   2. b   3. c   4. c   5. a

E. Functional Phrases/Transcript

Receptionist:	Advanced Technologies. **May I help you?**
Blake:	Yes. **This is** Charles Blake of Yamashita Limited. **I'd like to speak with** Mike Epstein, please.
Receptionist:	Just a minute and I'll put you through.
Epstein:	Hello Mr. Blake.
Blake:	Hello Mr. Epstein. **How are you?**
Epstein:	**I'm fine thanks.** How are you?
Blake:	Great.
Epstein:	Uh, when did you get in to San Francisco?
Blake:	Well I just arrived at my hotel a few moments ago.
Epstein:	Oh, uh, well **when should we** get together?
Blake:	I was wondering **if we could possibly** arrange a meeting for tomorrow sometime.
Epstein:	**Yes, that's fine.** I'll be free after eleven o'clock. **How's that?**
Blake:	Ah, that sounds fine with me.
Epstein:	Okay, uh, well, where are you staying?
Blake:	Well I'm staying at the Hilton Hotel.
Epstein:	All right that's very close to here. I'll tell you what, I'll meet you around eleven fifteen and then we can go out for lunch, and then I'll show you around the city.
Blake:	Okay, that would be very nice.
Epstein:	Okay, **one more thing** . . . uh, one of our, **I'd like to** introduce you to one of our Vice-Presidents, uh, Ms. Shirley Graham. She's in charge of the project that I'm working on. Uh, I was wondering **if we could** get together, uh, say on Wednesday.
Blake:	Ah-h, I have no plans on Wednesday, and I would like to meet her.
Epstein:	Okay then, if you could keep your schedule free uh around lunchtime on Wednesday, then I'll finalize that appointment with her.
Blake:	Okay, very good.
Epstein:	Okay, very good. I'll be looking forward to seeing you tomorrow morning.
Blake:	Tomorrow at 11:15 at the hotel.
Epstein:	Yes, okay.
Blake:	I'm looking forward to seeing you too.
Epstein:	Okay, see you then.
Blake:	Good-bye.
Epstein:	Bye-bye.

F. Supplementary Exercises

Variation 1: Functional Phrases/Transcript

Bliss:	Webber Industries, may I help you?
Milton:	Yes. **This is Bob Milton.**
Bliss:	This is Sam Bliss speaking. How are you Mr. Milton?

Milton:	**Fine and you?**
Bliss:	Just fine, thank you.
Milton:	I'm calling to see if we can arrange a meeting. There are several matters I'd like to discuss with you.
Bliss:	Okay, when would be convenient?
Milton:	**Could we meet tomorrow?**
Bliss:	Yes, that's possible. What time would be convenient?
Milton:	**How about 2:30?**
Bliss:	Fine. I'm looking forward to seeing you.
Milton:	Me too. Okay, in your office at 2:30 tomorrow, right?
Bliss:	Right. See you then.
Milton:	See you tomorrow.

Variation 2: Functional Phrases/Transcript

Receptionist:	Webber Industries, **can I help you?**
Milton:	**Yes. This is Bob Milton** from Myer's Shipping Company. **Could I speak with Mr. Webber, please?**
Receptionist:	**I'm afraid** Mr. Webber is not here right now. Can I take a message?
Milton:	Yes. Could you please ask Mr. Webber to call me back before 5:00 today?
Receptionist:	Yes sir. **Would you please spell your last name?**
Milton:	Certainly. M - I - L - T - O - N.
Receptionist:	**Could I have your telephone number please?**
Milton:	Yes. 877-3088.

EPISODE 3: Confirming Plans

B. General Comprehension

1. F   2. F   3. T   4. F   5. T

C. Detailed Listening

1. b   2. a   3. b   4. b   5. c

E. Functional Phrases/Transcript

Graham:	Come in.
Epstein:	Oh, Shirley, **do you have a minute?**
Graham:	Sure. Come on in Mike. **Have a seat.**
Epstein:	Oh, thanks. Listen, **I just wanted to let you know** that I've made reservations for lunch tomorrow afternoon around 12:15. Okay?
Graham:	With Mr. Blake?
Epstein:	**That's right**, of Yamashita Limited.

Graham: Okay. So, we should leave here at . . .?
Epstein: About 12:00.
Graham: 12:00 **sounds just fine**.
Epstein: Okay, good. I'll pick you up here at 12:00 and we can go over to his hotel together.
Graham: All right.
Epstein: Okay.
Graham: Now, have you already discussed any of the project with him?
Epstein: Yes, I did. I had an excellent meeting with him this afternoon.
Graham: And did you tell him that my main concerns are this October deadline and also the fact that they have no aftersales service in the States?
Epstein: Yes, I did and again I was very impressed with his flexibility and his . . . **I think** that we can work things out with him.
Graham: Okay. As long as its clear to both of you that it has to be worked out, and before October, because that's our deadline.
Epstein: Well, again, **I understand your reservations** Shirley, but again the technology of their product is really excellent. **I think** we really have to go ahead with this.
Graham: Yes. All right. Well, **let's discuss it further tomorrow**. All right?
Epstein: Okay. All right. Thank you. We'll see you tomorrow.
Graham: We'll see you around 12:00.
Epstein: Okay.

F. Supplementary Exercises

Variation I: Answers/Transcript

1./e   2./c   3./a   4./b   5./d

Powers: Excuse me. Do you have a minute?
Malone: Certainly. Please come in.
Powers: Thanks. I made an appointment for us to see Mr. Myers. Are you still free at 11:00 on Wednesday?
Malone: 11:00 on Wednesday? I'm afraid not. I'm busy all morning.
Powers: That's too bad.
Malone: How about 1:00 on Friday?
Powers: That's fine with me.
Malone: Would you call him back and see if Friday is good for him?
Powers: Sure. I'll call him right away.
Malone: Thanks.

Variation 2: Transcript

Myers: Hello. This is Bob Myers speaking.
Powers: Hello. This is Sandra Powers from Delta Electronics. I'm sorry but Mr. Malone is busy on Wednesday. If it's convenient for you, could we change our appointment to 1:00 on Friday?
Myers: I understand that you're very busy but Friday is too late. We have some very

serious problems. I think we should meet as soon as possible.

Powers:	I see. Could I call you back later today? I want to check our schedule for Thursday.
Myers:	Good. I'll be expecting your call later today.

EPISODE 4: An Important Introduction

B. General Comprehension

1. T   2. F   3. F   4. T   5. F

C. Detailed Listening

1. b   2. b   3. b   4. b   5. a

E. Functional Phrases/Transcript

Epstein:	Now, let's see. Where is he? Oh, there he is over there reading the newspaper.
Graham:	Uh huh.
Epstein:	Mr. Blake!
Blake:	Oh, hi Mike. **How are you** today?
Epstein:	Oh, **it's good to see you** Charles. **This is** our Vice-President, Shirley Graham. Shirley, **this is** Charles Blake from Yamashita Ltd.
Graham:	**It's nice to meet you** Mr. Blake.
Blake:	**Pleased to meet you** Ms. Graham.
Graham:	**How are you today?**
Blake:	**Fine. And you?**
Graham:	Just fine. Mike tells me that you . . . he took you around San Francisco yesterday.
Blake:	Yeah. We had a great time yesterday. We went down to Fisherman's Wharf and we had lunch and then we drove around San Francisco and saw a bit of the city.
Graham:	Is this your first trip to the West Coast?
Blake:	Well, not really. I was here about seven years ago. Just for a very brief visit and now I have a little bit more time to see some of the city.
Epstein:	Well, **I hate to interrupt** but we have a car outside and we have reservations at 12:15. So **why don't we** get over to the restaurant and we can continue our conversation there.
Graham:	Okay.
Epstein:	Okay?
Blake and Epstein:	**That sounds fine** to me.
Epstein:	Okay. **Let's go!**

F. Supplementary Exercises

Variation 1: Functional Phrases/Transcript

Powers: Mr. Myers?
Myers: Yes. **That's right.**
Powers: **I'm** Sandra Powers. I work with Mr. Malone.
Myers: Mrs. Powers. **How do you do?** I've been looking forward to meeting you.
Powers: **It's nice to meet you.** Mr. Myers. You've come a very long way on this trip so I hope things are going well. Welcome to San Francisco!

Variation 2: Functional Phrases/Transcript

Powers: Mr. Myers?
X: **Excuse me?**
Powers: **Are you** Mr. Myers from Dover Limited?
X: No, **I'm afraid not. Why don't you** ask reception to page him?
Powers: Oh, thank you. I'll do that. **Sorry to bother you.**
X: Oh, **not at all.**

EPISODE 5:   A Business Lunch

B. General Comprehension

1. F   2. F   3. T   4. F   5. T

C. Detailed Listening

1. c   2. spare parts; maintenance   3. b   4. quantity; size   5. done business

E. Functional Phrases/Transcript

Epstein: Well, that was a pretty good meal.
Graham: Um, it was delicious.
Epstein: **Would anyone like** some . . . some more coffee? Shirley?
Graham: **Not for me.** No thank you.
Blake: Yes. **I'd like** a little bit more please.
Epstein: Okay. There's the waiter. Waiter, **could we** have another cup of coffee over here please. Thank you.
Blake: Okay. Ms. Graham, **let me see if I understand you** correctly on this. Now, your basic problem is that we at Yamashita can not provide adequate maintenance or spare parts quickly enough.
Graham: Yes. **That's right.** That's my main concern.
Blake: Okay. Now you've rejected the proposal that we use your warehouse for storage space for spare parts.

9

Graham: Well, **not entirely**, Mr. Blake. **Let me clarify** that a little. Space is limited and it would depend very much on the quantity of parts, the size etcetera. **I would** need a lot more detail on that.

Blake: I can certainly understand your concerns. I'm going to put this information in a report after I telex Tokyo.

Graham: Okay.

Blake: And **I'll have** the report ready for you tomorrow. And maybe we can come up with a solution to the problem.

Graham: Okay. Well, that sounds fine. **Even then** Mr. Blake, I can't make any guarantees. You know we've never done business with a Japanese company before so it's quite an undertaking.

Blake: Oh, certainly I can understand.

Graham: So I hope you will understand.

Blake: Sure.

Graham: Okay.

F. Supplementary Exercises

Functional Phrases/Transcript

Davis: **To summarize**, there are still problems with the delivery date and the size of the discount, but **everything else** is okay, is that right?

Jones: Yes. **That's right**. The price is higher than we expected, and we need delivery within six months at the latest.

Davis: I see. Well, **I'll see what I can do**. The delivery date is going to be a problem, but **I'll check** and see if it's possible. **Can we get together** again? **How about** later this week?

Jones: Okay, but **I'm afraid** I won't be free **except for** tomorrow afternoon. **Is that too early?**

Davis: No, that'll be fine. How about 3:00?

Jones: Okay, good. I'll see you tomorrow, Mr. Davis.

Davis: See you then.

EPISODE 6: The Disagreement

B. General Comprehension

1. T   2. T   3. F   4. T   5. F

C. Detailed Listening

1. b   2. b   3. a   4. c   5. b

E. Functional Phrases/Transcript

Graham: . . . Yes, in Japan. The quality of their product is extremely good but I don't know anything about their reliability. Can they be relied on to do this by October 1st? **You know** we've worked with United Industries before and **I think we should** just go ahead on the deal with them. **I feel sure** that they can have everything installed and working by October 1st.

Epstein: Well, look, **but there's another argument**, Shirley, and that is that **I agree with you** they haven't established themselves in the States **but** that's an advantage. . . . that's our advantage because we can get their technology before other companies can. If we're willing to take the risk. **I think we really have to** take that risk.

Graham: Well, **I think** that's basically what it comes down to Mike. You want to take the risk and I really am not willing to. **I don't feel** that I can afford to take the risk.

Epstein: Oh, but what have I been doing for the last year? I've been looking for the new technology to really make this factory something special and I think that this is what we need to do. **I can't understand why** you disagree with this. It's very clear.

Graham: And I think **you've done a very good job** but **I think** that . . . there are more disadvantages than advantages. And **I'm sorry but I'm afraid** on this you're just not going to be able to have it the way you want it . . .

F. Supplementary Exercises

Variation: Answers/Transcript

1./b   2./c   3./a   4./d

Malone: I think we should hire John Hart. He has ten years of experience and he's 35 years old, quite mature. What do you think?

Powers: I don't agree. I think we should hire Kevin Ward. He's much better educated and very bright.

Malone: Yes, he does have an M.B.A. degree, but he doesn't have any real job experience.

Powers: That's true, but Mr. Hart has only four years' experience in sales.

Malone: Yes, that's a good point. Maybe we need more information. Let's talk with them both again.

Powers: Do you really think that's necessary? A second interview is a good idea, but I don't think we have the time. I think we really have to decide today.

Malone: Well, I agree, time is a problem. But this new position is very important. We can wait one more day. Would you mind calling them back?

Powers: All right. I'll try to schedule them both for tomorrow afternoon.

EPISODE 7: Keeping in touch

B. General Comprehension

1. F   2. T   3. F   4. T   5. F

C. Detailed Listening
1. c   2. b   3. b   4. a   5. b

E. Functional Phrases/Transcript

Epstein: Well, **it's too bad** but **I guess** things worked out the way we thought they might.

Blake: Yeah, but this has been a valuable experience for us. Now we know what our biggest problem will be with the North American market.

Epstein: Well **for me**, of course, I'm still not happy. **I think** that your machinery is the best on the market. **It's just too bad** that I . . . we couldn't convince Shirley. **Still**, I can understand her point too. She's under a lot of pressure here to get this . . . this new operation going by October.

Blake: Sure.

Epstein: Well listen, what are your plans from here?

Blake: Well, tomorrow I'm flying to New York in the afternoon to meet with some prospective customers.

Epstein: Well, I certainly wish you the best of luck out there.

Blake: Well, thank you.

Epstein: Also, **I'd like to ask**, **if you just could** keep in touch later. I'm very interested to know what happens. In the future, you know, we never know what's going to happen but **it may be possible** for us to work together.

Blake: Okay, **I certainly will** Mike.

Epstein: One other thing. **What are you doing** this afternoon?

Blake: Well, I have no plans.

Epstein: Well, I remember the nice game of golf that we had together when I was in Tokyo. I have a membership in a golf club just across the Bay here and I've made some reservations. **Would you like to join me** in a round of golf this afternoon?

Blake: **That sounds like a great idea**. Sure.

Epstein: Good the weather's fine.

Blake: Okay. Let's go.

Epstein: Yeah. I'd just love to get out of this office today.

Blake: Great.

Epstein: Let's go.

F. Supplementary Exercises

Functional Phrases/Transcript

Winthrop: **Would you like** (I'd like to invite you) to see our factory while you are in New York. I think you will find it quite interesting and . . .

Vale: That's very kind of you. **Unfortunately**, (But I'm afraid) my schedule is booked up all next week. I'm meeting with several different companies while I'm here.

Winthrop: **I'm sorry to hear that.** (That's too bad.) Well, **I'd like to keep in touch.** (Let's keep in touch.) I may be in London early next year and . . .

Vale: Please give me a ring then.

Winthrop:	Thank you. **I certainly will**. (I'll do that.) Well, it's nearly 12:30. **Are you free** (Why don't you join me) for lunch?
Vale:	**I'm afraid I'm not**. (I'm sorry but) I have other plans for this afternoon but **I appreciate the invitation**. (Thank you anyway.)
Winthrop:	**My pleasure**. (Not at all.) Perhaps another time.

EPISODE 8: New Customer

B. General Comprehension

1. F   2. T   3. F   4. T   5. F

C. Detailed Listening

1. b   2. c   3. a   4. b   5. b

E. Functional Phrases/Transcript

Receptionist:	Good morning sir, **can I help you?**
Blake:	Yeah, **I have an appointment** to see Mr. Chapman, Stewart Chapman at 10:30.
Receptionist:	Oh, Mr. Chapman. **Can I have your name please?**
Blake:	Yeah, **the name** is uh Blake, Charles Blake of Yamashita Limited.
Receptionist:	All right, thank you. Just a moment please . . . Yes, there's a Mr. Blake here to see Mr. Chapman . . . Oh, I see, thank you . . . Uh, Mr. Blake, I'm sorry, Mr. Chapman is not here today.
Blake:	Uh-huh . . .
Receptionist:	Uh, but there's a Mr. Gomez who can come talk to you. Would you take a chair and wait for a moment?
Blake:	Okay, sure. Thank you.
Receptionist:	Thank you.
Gomez:	Good morning Mr. Blake. **Welcome to** Federal Motors. My name is Dave Gomez.
Blake:	**Pleased to meet you** Mr. Gomez.
Gomez:	**Nice to meet you** sir. Did you have a good trip to New York?
Blake:	Yeah, and I'm looking forward to staying here a few days and doing some business.
Gomez:	Great. Uh, Mr. Chapman **asked me to apologize to you**. He was called out of town on a personal matter very suddenly. And he does assure me that he is looking forward to meeting with you as soon as he returns.
Blake:	Uh-huh.
Gomez:	In the meantime I'm quite familiar with Yamashita and uh your products and uh, so **I'd like to** work with you **if that would be all right?**
Blake:	Okay, sure. And **I understand** about Mr. Chapman's absence. **It's no problem.**

Gomez: Okay, great. Uh, well you must be tired from your trip, so **why don't we** go into the office and sit down and relax for a few minutes and we can get some coffee or tea **if you'd like?**

Blake: Okay, that sounds great.

Gomez: Great.

F. Supplementary Exercises

Variation: Functional Phrases/Transcript

Malone: **Hello.**

Powers: Hello Bill. Sorry to call you at home.

Malone: **No problem. What can I do for you?**

Powers: I'm afraid I've got a problem. My mother is quite ill and I have to fly to Miami today. I hate to ask, but would you mind meeting Bob Myers of Dover Limited, tomorrow?

Malone: **I'm sorry to hear about your mother. I'd be happy to help out. What time do you expect Mr. Myers to arrive?**

Powers: He'll be there at 10:30.

Malone: **Okay, I'll meet him then.**

Powers: Thanks! Again, I'd like to apologize for this inconvenience.

Malone: **Don't worry about it. I'll take care of everything here and I certainly hope your mother is feeling better.**

Powers: Thank you. I hope I can be back by Wednesday, but I'm just not sure right now.

Malone: **Sure I understand.**

Powers: Thanks again. I appreciate it. I'll call you tomorrow afternoon around 4:00.

Malone: **Fine. I'll talk with you then.**

EPISODE 9: Negotiations

B. General Comprehension

1. F   2. F   3. T   4. F   5. T

C. Detailed Listening

1. b   2. b   3. b   4. c   5. c

E. Functional Phrases/Transcript

Gomez: Uh when we first put these machines in operation, install them in our factories, can you send over a group of technical advisors who speak English and could train our engineers and workmen?

Blake: Certainly. **In fact** we have some engineers in a language training program now and they could come over within a few months and be available any time you need them.

Gomez: Great, great, that sounds good. Another one of our major concerns is the service manual. We're quite concerned about getting a service manual in English that will be easy to read and very clear and useful for our engineers.

Blake: Yeah, again, **as I told you** we are preparing a translation of the Japanese manual we have now, and we expect that to be ready in a short time.

Gomez: **By** short time . . . **could you give me** an estimate?

Blake: Uh, **I'd like to say** two weeks, **but I'd have to get back to you**, but probably about two or three weeks.

Gomez: Oh, that sounds **quite reasonable. As you know** we have until January 1st to actually install these machines and get them operating, so we're under no deadline pressure here.

Blake: Okay, well that gives us a fair amount of time to work with.

Gomez: Plenty of time. That sounds good Mr. Blake. Uh, another concern is your professional record, uh performance record in Japan with these machines.

Blake: **Why don't I** send you some reports that we have on the performance of the robot in some Japanese companies who are also our clients. And **I'm sure** you'll be quite pleased with what you see.

Gomez: Okay, great. **Could you** get those off to me within a few weeks?

Blake: Sure. **That shouldn't be a problem. In fact** as soon as I get back to Tokyo **I'll see to it.**

Gomez: Excellent. Thank you very much.

Blake: **Is there anything else?**

Gomez: Well, no. That covers all the major points.

Blake: Okay. Fine.

Gomez: Sounds good . . .

F. Supplementary Exercises

Variation I: Functional Phrases/Transcript

Myers: **Hello, this is Bob Myers speaking.**

Powers: Bob? This is Sandra Powers.

Myers: **Oh, Sandra, how are you?**

Powers: Well that's why I'm calling you. There have been a few changes here, and I wanted to let you know.

Myers: **What kind of changes?**

Powers: Well, Bill Malone has resigned, and I've been put in charge of our project.

Myers: **Well, I'm sorry to hear about Bill Malone, but congratulations to you.**

Powers: Thank you. But that's not all. I'm still interested in getting your machines for our new factory, and I've been able to extend the deadline a month, to November 1st. Do you think you can make it?

Myers: **Well, if you can accept my earlier proposal, I don't see any problem.**

Powers: When are you flying back to Tokyo?

Myers: **Tomorrow morning.**

Powers: **Could you** change your flight and stop by here for a day or two?

Myers: **Let me check with my office in Tokyo first, then I'll get back to you.**

Powers: Good. **If you could** call me back within a couple of hours and let me know, **I'd appreciate it.**

Myers: **Well our office in Tokyo isn't open for another four hours, so** . . .

Powers: Right. I forgot about the time difference . . .

Variation 2: Transcript

Myers: Yes? This is Bob Myers speaking.

Powers: Hello Bob. This is Sandra Powers calling.

Myers: Oh, Sandra, it's good to hear from you. What's up?

Powers: Well, to begin with, I've decided to leave Delta Electronics and join another company. I've been thinking about it for quite a while now, and last week I was offered a position at Data Systems Inc.

Myers: Well, congratulations.

Powers: Thanks. But the reason I'm calling you is that I'll be working on a project very similar to the one I was working on before, and there's a good chance that we'll be interested in your machines.

Myers: Well, that's great news. I'll be looking forward to hearing from you.

Powers: If you could keep me informed of any new developments, I'd really appreciate it.

Myers: I'll certainly do that.

Powers: How did things go in New York?

Myers: Well we just finished our meeting, and things look very good. They like our machines, and there are no serious problems. Some of their people will fly to Tokyo the week after next, and if things work out, I'm pretty sure we'll get our first big order in North America. I'm very pleased.

Powers: Well, congratulations. Next time we get together, we'll have to celebrate.

Myers: Sounds good Sandra. Maybe we'll even get in a round of golf.

Powers: Good idea. Well, have a good trip back to Tokyo, Bob.

Myers: Thanks for calling, Sandra, and good luck with your new job.

Sandra: Thanks.

8. _____   Right. I forgot about the time difference . . .

    _____

    _____

VARIATION 2

Myers receives a telephone call in his hotel room late Wednesday afternoon. Listen to the dialog once, and answer the following questions.

1.   What happened to Sandra Powers?
2.   Why is she calling?
3.   Who is going to fly to Tokyo the week after next? Why?

G. Group Practice

Role-play the variations. Myers' situation is the same in both, but Sandra Powers' situation is different. Myers must listen carefully.

Picture Acknowledgements
The photographs at the head of Episodes 1 and 2, and on the cover, were
not taken in the San Francisco Hilton Hotel, but we are grateful to the Hilton
management for help and advice. We would like to thank Briggens
House Hotel for allowing us to use their premises for photographs on
pages 19 and 36. The photographs on pages 14, 25, 30, 42, 47 and 58
were taken at the Longman Group. The photograph on page 52 is copyright
Picturepoint-London.

The cover photograph was taken in the lobby at Terminus House, Harlow
Town Centre.

All photographs by Con Putbrace.

Illustrated by Richard Bonson.